I0019210

"Dominate the market in the age of AI"

The

Addictive

Experience

Build an addictive website/app that users love,

share & never want to leave.

Mahir Iram

Index

Why Should You Read This Book?

Dear Founders, Innovators & Designers

Design is not just what it looks like and feels like. Design is how it works. **- Steve Jobs (1995 - 2011)**

*T*his is the best time in the history of humankind for entrepreneurs, founders, designers, creators, and creative folks like you to start offering their creative services or create a unique money generating idea to billions of users through apps or websites. **It doesn't matter if you use AI tools or a team of designers & developers or if you are building by yourself.**

Now it is even easier because all those popular AI tools let you build an app only by command, a powerful invention by humankind which did not exist before.

There is one big exception though. Almost no ideas are unique and almost nothing attracts visitors now and that exception, my friend, is going to make you the luckiest person alive or the unluckiest.

If you think you have a great business idea and all you need is one cool website or app for it, and to run some Ads for people to rush to your website/app, then you are wrong. Maybe it was possible in 2015 or 2020. But not anymore. No ideas are unique anymore and people don't have enough attention span to visit your website or app, even if they do, they usually leave as soon as they visit.

The internet is full of all those unique e-commerce websites, unique pet apps that also have socializing options with other pet owners, cutting edge SAAS tools, unique online travel portals that use an algorithm to match you with the cheapest hotel while helping you share your rent with another fellow traveller, email marketing SAAS software that leverages AI, social media for traveling professionals, "unique" AI-based chat app that also helps improve writing skill of its users, mindfulness & yoga app where you can also chat with an AI assistant who will listen to your mental health problems and try to cheer you up and many more different apps/websites.

Do you understand what I am trying to say?

Well, get this, everything that is possible to be created on the internet has already been created. Now that people have access to AI tools and as a result, making apps or websites is not a matter of skill set now, it's just a matter of people "wishing" about it and boom! it's there.

Take a moment to grasp the idea.

No matter how unique your features are, either these will already be available in the market, therefore, hold no point of attraction for your visitors OR the internet giants in your market will replicate your "unique" features and will do a better job than you and win the crowds even before you make your apps bug free from your early users' feedback.

So what's the solution?

I will tell you the solution in this book

This solution not only makes your visitors stay at your app/website for a long period of time, it also hooks your visitors to your digital product so much that they keep coming back. **The best part is you can be a complete beginner and still you can apply the secrets shared in this book.**

This situation is also true for your competitors and guess what? Most of your competitors' apps / websites are failing to stand out too and that my friend, opens a door for you to shine and stand out.

Understand this, "Unique features" doesn't work anymore. **"Unique experience" does** (which 99% of the existing apps and websites fail to achieve.)

You need to create a magical experience for your visitors.

An experience that they will never find in the other apps on the internet. The experience will be so addicting to them that they will keep coming back to your website/app. There is a specific secret and art to achieve this with your digital product and in this book I am going to talk about these.

I will discuss in detail how you can create a magical user experience that hooks your visitors to your website and app which results in more signups, downloads, orders, actions and site visits etc.

Eventually, your app or website will be part of their daily life, they will come back again and again, like they are addicted to your website/app.

If you want to know how, I invite you to mindfully read this book.

Why Should You Read This Book?

You are here, because:

1. You are a new founder and you have an app or website business idea, and you want to get enough signups / downloads / orders / tractions etc. in your digital product (app / website or anything digitally accessible) OR

2. You are not a new founder and you already started with your app / website business and now you want to offer something "more" to your visitors that makes them keep coming back to your website/app.

(Note: Even if you already have a large user base from your website or app business, you still need to read this book because, for you, the opportunity for growth is enormous. What I am about to share is almost not shared anywhere in public and is very crucial for founders & product designers.)

Whether you are in B2C or B2B business, whether you are a SAAS company or not, whether you are in e-commerce or Education or Finance or Healthcare or Gaming or Real Estate or Retail or Agro or Social Media or Travel & Tourism or Dating or Fitness or Logistics & Transportation or Mindfulness **or** whether you are making an aggregator site that connects service providers with service seekers or maybe you are just creating your portfolio website or an agency website or maybe you are offering productivity tool for entrepreneurs or marketers, **whether you are making AI apps/sites you need to read this.**

It doesn't matter what industry you are in or what type of apps or websites you are building.

In this book, I am going to share how you can defeat mediocrity in your app/website no matter what type of app it is and what industry you operate in. I am going to share some brain-hacking UX tactics that create an **EXPERIENCE** that directly influences the subconscious mind of visitors, which is connected to the deepest psychology of your users' behavior that eventually makes them addicted to your digital product whether it is a mobile app or a website or anything digitally accessible.

In this book, I am going to share those UX secrets that connect to the deepest emotions and desires of the visitors and make them fall in love with your app that they have no other way but to sign up (or take any desirable action) and **become loyal customer to what you are offering regardless of the type of business you are in. PERIOD.**

Just like they visit their favorite museums, restaurants, parks, or places and they visit the same place again and again, they will visit your website or app again and again for the experience you are offering and they will stay there as long as they possibly can.

It's like a drug, but I love to call it "art" or better "UX Art".

Once you achieve this, your website or app is not boring anymore. It becomes a place for good addiction, a place where your visitors come to find peace and they will use your app (& stay there) as long as they can. I will show you how.

See you in the next chapters.

The Cave Experience

Suppose you like adventures. You are in front of a cave and you don't have any idea where the cave leads. You stepped inside. The cave is full of darkness. You felt the whisper of the unknown. With it, came the heart-beating of horror that comes with the unknown and uncertainty. You realized you started shaking & sweating inside. You felt the need to run. However, since childhood, you have liked the unknown.

(Fig 1: The Cave Experience)

So, you took your first step inside the cave and suddenly you heard a very heart-shaking violent howling. That howling echoed multiple times and made the horror movie-like scene 10 times more life-threatening.

You became thrilled, scared, wanted to run, and still wanted to go further toward the deep darkness of the cave. That was your experience. We can call this "Cave's User Experience" or in short "Cave's UX".

Now, let's say, we have control over all the elements of the cave. We have the control to reduce the volume of the howling or fully remove that. We can also control the darkness level if we want. Even if we want, we can add some earthquake effects in the cave that can make your environment more hostile.

Or we can make the situation more pleasant by adding a sunlight source, removing the howling, and adding some friendly animals like squirrels around. By changing the natural elements, we are changing the Cave's User Experience.

You see, like the cave, your website and/or app has an experience. We can change color, button position, text style, layout, etc. to change your emotional response. However, there is a science to apply this knowledge. With proper application of this knowledge, it is possible that you can increase your sign-up and retention rate.

And if you can create some "addictive" experience that connects to your visitors' deep-rooted emotions, you can get a few percent of people among your visitors who will keep coming back.

Once you get those few percent of people who keep coming back, the rest of the work is just to do the marketing, eventually that few percent will become MILLIONS of users. You will make history.

The problem is, UX can't be seen. It is felt.

That's why, most of the founders/entrepreneurs and even designers fail to apply it properly because they emphasize on the visual part which is a common mistake.

The internet is full of promising applications and websites which are visually world class. They still fail because of the "experience" they are offering.

We need to avoid that.

CHAPTER 1

3 Fatal Mistakes Founders Make With Their App/Web Based Business

*Most people spend more time and energy going around problems than in trying to solve them.. - **Henry Ford (1863 - 1947)***

*I*t is not hard to guess that you as a founder are very visionary. You are very excited to kick-start your dream business. Like any logical & smart entrepreneur, your goal is simple: spend as little time and money as possible and get as many customers/users as you can.

It doesn't matter whether you just started or have already started a year or two years ago. Your struggles are many. Below are the struggles you face as a founder:

- **Hiring the right team**. Which is a non-stop job. No matter how hard you try, you can never hire the right team for your business.

- **Making the app ready for the market.** No matter how hard you try, the app is never market-ready. Today you are dealing with feature A and fixing bug number #323 and tomorrow you realize feature A is not gonna work and working on bug number #102. And suddenly there is a new programming language or technology in the market. Now you are not even sure if you hired the right programmer.

- If you have investors or potential investors, well done. Now 10 times the pressure and stress.

- You have a small customer base and all of the customers are asking for different features. There is one good customer though, except that customer is not ready to pay you.

- Somehow, after many trials and errors, you've managed to get a good number of paying customers and then one day, you are shocked by seeing the server bill. Now you have to optimize your backend programs so that your online business takes minimum storage & uses minimum database transactions. You realize, the Netflix TV series "Silicon Valley" was not even 1% inaccurate.

- No matter what, you can't fixate on one idea/business model. You seem to change your business model and app idea very often. It becomes even more expensive when your developers already built the app.

Well, I can keep on writing, and no matter what, the list of struggles you face will never end.

You keep facing problems after one another.

With every new problem you face, it eats your energy and budget. If you are thinking "OMG! This guy is exactly describing my current situation now. How can he tell that?" Well, don't be surprised. Sadly, I've come across everything I mentioned and wasted 4 years of my valuable time and energy by learning very expensive (cost $400k) lessons.

I was stupid and foolish enough to think that, "One day, these will go away". Well, you are right to think that they didn't go away. Problems actually never go away, unless you do something fundamentally differently. I will share that with you soon.

I read a lot of books to learn, to improve and to find if there were any mistakes I had been making.

I actually read 100+ books. Books on marketing, growth, team management, entrepreneurship, you name it. Eventually, I started thinking I had spiritual problems. "you have to find your why", "you have to heal your past traumas", "heal your heart chakra", "you are not vibrating at a high frequency" etc. So, I read tons of spiritual books as well.

I was hurting. Then, one day, I realized the mistakes I was making.

I also noticed that all the founders are making the same mistakes too. The books I read somehow gave me hints, clues and tips for those mistakes. I came to realize some unique & different perspectives, which I would like to add to all my learnings from different books.

With my utmost humility, I want to credit all those writers, coaches & startup mentors out there and also all those smart YouTuber entrepreneurs whose continuous efforts eventually helped me overcome my situation. And now, I am fortunate to share my perspective.

My perspective is divided into two parts, the first part is:

> *All the challenges, problems, and stresses founders face are symptoms of the founder making some mistakes somewhere.*

Meaning, if you are struggling, you are making mistakes somewhere which you don't know. Simple, but very powerful.

The second part of the perspective is this:

> *There are 3 fatal mistakes responsible for most of the struggles. If a founder solves those mistakes, most of the problems will be solved.*

Big promise! Most of the problems will be solved!

I know it may sound unrealistic. If all the problems can be explained by only 3 mistakes, "Why are not founders becoming careful then?" you may think, and "Why is nobody talking about this by now?"

Well, first of all, it is "my" big promise. I learned this the hard way, after struggling for 4 years, wasting around $400k. So, I am the one who figured this out. Once I learned, I couldn't stop myself from thinking, "It was this easy but for an average founder (not a fool like me who takes 4 years) to figure this out, s/he has to spend around a year??".

I can't let that happen and that's why I wrote this book.

Let's get back to the point, you might be wondering, "well what are those 3 mistakes?", let me share the 3 mistakes first and then let me explain how it can solve 99% of your early problems (& stresses) and save 2-4 years or at least 1 year of your life. Thank me later. Deal?

Here are the 3 mistakes:

1. **Not following UX processes in the beginning** - and as a result of that, founders fail in the early launches. With the hope of spending less and getting customers quickly, they actually spend more money and more time and hardly get any customers or get very less customers than their

competitors.

2. **Hiring developers too quickly** - Developers are expensive. Because, in the early processes, decisions change a lot. Every decision change results in additional development costs.

3. **Hiring a UI designer who hardly does any UX process** - This mistake falls under the "Wrong hiring" category. No matter how beautiful the UI of your website or app looks, it doesn't matter if the designer is not involved in the UX process. Eventually, visitors won't stay and your business will hurt.

Now, let's dive deep into how these 3 mistakes are involved with all the early problems. After that, I will also share how you can solve these problems and eventually grow your customer base by 2x/10x/30x more than you actually would and the best part is you won't have to spend any additional money to achieve this growth, in fact, you will actually save money while solving the mistakes.

Who wouldn't want to give it a try if something has the potential to solve their problem and as a bonus get more growth? while saving money?

Let's talk about this in the next sections of this chapter!

Mistake 1: Which Sabotages Your Growth Permanently.

Let's talk about the first mistake and how it is creating all the other problems in your life.

Not following UX processes in the beginning:

Let me share a very interesting real-business story.

It was 1960. A "popular" car company decided to launch a new car model for the US market.

They observed the market, conducted surveys, and discovered that, among the new car purchases, 46% were done by the younger generation. Most of them were single, college-going students. This was very interesting data but the company had the risk of targeting too small a market if the company only pursued that small group as their primary target customer.

They researched more and discovered that most of the families in the US were buying a second car and women had the purchasing power for that. Women liked small-sized cars because of their parking ability and mobility. On the other hand, the college-going younger generations were also interested in luxurious small-sized cars.

The younger men liked to feel the rawness of the street and research showed they liked to feel closer to the street.

With all this research, the company decided on some of the features:

1. The car should be small. The seat should be very low in height to give the passengers a closer feel to the road.

2. A debate went on whether the car should be a 2-seater car or a 4-seater car. Well, from the research, it looked like most of the people from the target group were interested in a 2-seater car but that would take away the opportunity to sell to the masses as well. Eventually, they decided on 4-seating arrangements while keeping the sporty and luxurious look intact.

The company created some possible car models and invited a group of couples having small babies (who were completely out of their primary target group). They showed their car design and asked for their opinions. When asked, "Would you buy this car?"

most of the couples said no they were not interested (Big surprise, isn't it?).

Then they were asked to guess the price of the car. The couple groups gave their answers and the interviewer revealed the actual price. After knowing the price, the team witnessed that most of the couples were coming with various justifications expressing their interest to purchase the car.

What happened was, after hearing the price, most of the couples became interested in most of the cases. Actually, the luxurious and sporty look of the car gave the couple the impression that the car was too expensive and they couldn't afford it. That's why they didn't show much interest at the beginning.

But once they actually learnt that the car was not that expensive, those same couple groups wanted to buy the car.

That gave the team further insights about the car:

"The car should be affordable and less costly"

This point made sense because their primary target group was college-going students who had very limited financial resources.

The company hired a few (5-7) car design agencies to come up with possible design models of the car and shared their findings and eventually the management of the company selected one best design.

On April 17, 1964, in front of a large media contingent at the New York World's Fair, the press conference of the car launch took place. The Ford Mustang Mania (now you know, what I was talking about) spread worldwide. It became one of the top-selling cars in history with a record of selling more than 100,000 cars within only 4 months after launch.

See, for Ford's case, the market was already filled with diversified types of cars. At that time, the popular cars were Beetles, Nash Rambler, and Studebaker Lark. Still, the Mustang won the crowd. They hacked their way towards their target customer by doing proper research which gave them key information. It's very powerful yet most of the founders avoid it.

You may be wondering, well what does this story have to do with my app or website business. Here is the catch, in the UX Process, there is a research step called "UX Research". When the Ford team asked different groups of couples to have a look at the design of the car, they asked many questions and made them sit in the car.

In fact, the Ford team did "UX research" on their car when they asked the couples to sit inside and use the car. The history just didn't mention the term "UX Research". It all went under the term called "Market Research".

Actually, all the successful startups/businesses do UX research, but when the press & media publish the news, they don't use the term "UX research" as this term is not widely known to the masses. Therefore, the importance of UX research was never felt, and only giant & serious tech companies do UX research.

Most of the new founders get busy with preparing pitch decks, financial models, hiring new recruits etc.

How ironic! The most crucial part of your business which can make or break your business gets the least or zero attention. This is a crime happening.

Even most of the UI/UX designers can't comprehend the idea that UX research is the most important part of launching a product. They just do basic competitive analysis, some user journey mapping, and many other documentation without ever feeling the level of power they hold deciding the future of the business.

That's why, I urge and request that you as a founder be involved in the UX process. In my experience, I have seen founders hiring market researchers or doing the research by themselves. The scary part is, in all the early market research phases, the UX research process is very rarely included.

If you are a UI&UX designer in your team, convince your stakeholders to allow more time in the UX research.

By doing market research, you can find the "Unique features" but not the "Unique experience". In order to find "Unique experience", one must conduct UX Research.

The market rewards extra-ordinarily for extraordinary user experiences. Remember this, all the time.

But Mahir, that was a car company. Any examples from tech companies?

Well, there are hundreds of success stories of tech startups who made billions once they did their UX research. Let me share a few:

Airbnb:

Started as an air mattress-selling company. By doing rigorous UX research and refining their problem, they are now a multi-billion dollar company revolutionizing the travel and hospital industry.

Dropbox:

Conducting extensive market research that focused on users' pain points Dropbox is now #1 cloud storage company.

Slack:

Gained popularity due to its easy intuitive user interface and seamless user experience. The founders understood the shortcomings of existing workspace tools.

The internet is full of such stories. You go to your favorite restaurants, because of the experience that restaurant offers. You go to your favorite park, because of the experience that park offers. You go to your loved one, because of the experience you get when you are with that person. Religious people go to church, temple & mosque because of the spiritual experience they get from there.

Fix the experience. You will fix the problem. It's that simple.

Let's take a look at the troubles you face when there is no proper UX process:

1. You are confused about the features. When you are confused about the features, you tend to have more in-team meetings and brainstorming sessions, and you struggle to find answers to all new questions.

   The worst part is, you don't even realize that you are in confusion. That, my friend, destroys your app's experience. Visitors also feel the tension by experiencing incomplete experience in your app/site and they usually leave after first sign up or visit.

2. Usually, when there is no UX process involved in the beginning, you just follow an existing app/site or follow inspirations and make the developers do the work. This sabotages your growth big times. Maybe this was possible before 2015 but not anymore.

3. When meeting investors, you fail to give them the right answers that would satisfy them. Investors are always skeptical. Their job is to doubt you. When you answer their questions, you know your answer is right, however, they don't feel it most of the time because they want to gain more clarity. Your "right answer" and investors' "right

answer" need to match. Sadly, it doesn't happen because you didn't have enough evidence to make them excited.

I can keep writing more. But hope you've got an idea. You may say, "but still, my company is growing and I didn't do any UX Research".

My answer would be, "Of course you are growing. That's not the point. The point is, how much MORE could you possibly grow, had you done UX Research? Let alone the discussions related to creating an addictive experience".

I will let you think about this for a moment before going to the next chapter that will show you how you could have saved thousands of dollars just by being more UX smart.

Mistake 2: Protect Yourself From This Mistake & I Will Show You More Money & Time

Let's talk about mistake 2 "**Hiring developers too quickly**".

Before that, let me share another story of mine.

It was 2015. Me and my co-founders, very excited to launch our new app which was a "Map Based Social Media", started looking for an Android & iOS Developer to build the app.

Sadly, we didn't do any proper UX research.

We were very confident, because we knew we had done enough market research that proved the point that more & more people are becoming interested in location-based apps. We had lucrative data showing X% of users now pivoting from Facebook & Instagram to different types of social media.

Y% of users are now more interested in location-based map-focused apps. Z% of users will literally jump into an app that provides location-based social media features.

Even interestingly, among X users, Y% of users love chatting features. We had no reason for being demotivated. Our passion was high, emotion was sky-touching and excitement was earth-shaking.

One thought never crossed our mind. That was "although the data was correct, our users may not love our app".

So we did what most of the early staged founders do. We hired developers. Since I was already a product designer, I knew our app would become world class.

After hiring developers, the biggest nightmare started.

The development became a never-ending process. Well, to be honest, development IS something which never ends. But not, when you have just started.

But we didn't know it back then.

After months of hard work with the developer (& of course spending a lot of money) we launched the app, only to realize that target users are not that much interested in the app. We threw an app launch party and asked all the attendees what they think about the app.

Every one of them said, "Wow, amazing app".

Then they went home. Never got back to the app. Maybe uninstalled the same night.

Saddest breakup story ever.

We, with full of courage, tried to "figure out" what was wrong. Guess what? we called the developers again (who charges hourly btw) and gave them new development tasks. This time, we knew what was the mistake (all in our mind though) and how to solve that.

This time too, development became a never ending process and new bugs kept coming out. More bugs kept coming out, more good news for the developer. Then, the second launch party. Again the same high hope and then we again realised, no it's not gonna work anymore.

"How about we run some ads?" one of my co-founders suggested. "Good idea, let's do it". So we did. We failed miserably again.

You may be thinking, how long have we been doing this "expensive" learning session?

Well, to be exact, for this app, 2 years. If you think, "What?? 2 years took you to grow?". Well, the answer is "No. Not to Grow. We needed 2 years to realise that, we should change the idea to something else".

Then we pivoted to another idea. This time, instead of "Location Based Social Media", we wanted to use the existing code infrastructure to create a "Field Force Monitoring Solution" which was a B2B SAAS app.

We needed additional 2 years of stupid learning and 2/3 pivot to make this business grow. That's another story. But here is the thing.

"Hiring developers too quickly" is a common mistake founders make. Founders want an asap launch and the only solution to them is "to hire a developer" for that and that, my friend is a trap.

For new founders with a new product, I get it, you want to launch ASAP. You have investors, you have timeline, market competition etc. etc. That pressure will trigger you to take the decision to hire developers as fast as you can.

But it's a paradox. Don't fall for this trap.

If you already have a running business app/website with existing users. This lesson is important for you too. Before shipping new features to an existing product, proper UX research needs to be done.

(Disclaimer: I am not against developers. In fact, early in my career, I have been a web developer myself. I have seen hundreds of projects being developed after months of coding and adding new features which eventually fail just because of lack of proper UX research. I believe a developer has the power to totally change the game, only if the right UX research is done. No hard feelings for developers. I know their struggle.)

First of all, why is it a mistake?

Here's why:

- When you've just started with your website or app project, your ideas/features will change a lot. Every feature change comes with extra development cost. Take time to figure out what users want before hiring a developer.

(If you already have a running app/website business, I believe you already have a developer or a group of developers in place. For your case, chances are high the UX process is happening without your knowledge. For new features, you should do proper UX research. You are lucky that you are reading this book. You have a chance to skyrocket your growth if you already have a regular user group. Keep reading.)

- When you are too much in the process of changing features, your app will tend to generate lots of bugs. Device compatibility issues will also increase resulting in more time and more development cost. Which you could have avoided by doing proper research.

- Market keeps bringing new programming languages for developers and you have the risk of falling in the trap of hiring a programmer/developer who is expert in that "new demanding" programming language and then one day, that programmer/developer will leave and you will have to find another programmer who is expert in the same stack.

  But suddenly, that "new demanding" programming language or technology is not new anymore and nobody is using this so you will struggle finding another programmer/developer skilled in the same stack of knowledge and technology.

Say, you have a $10K budget for an initial launch of your app or new feature (for existing app). You plan to spend 50% of it (which is $5K) for development and the rest of the 50% for doing marketing, branding etc. You will be lucky if you can finish the development within $5K and get a smooth launch that can attract both users and investors.

In most cases, founders fall into the trap of "Launching Early" and they keep spending money which in most of the cases even go beyond the total budget.

Founders spend money to fix & add new features. Those new features cost extra time & money. Also those new features create more new feature-needs and more bugs, resulting in more time & money. It's a paradox. I am surprised, hardly anyone talks about this very serious issue which can save thousands of dollars and hours.

Avoid this mistake, I will show you how you could have saved both your time & money. I will show you how you can spend a minimum amount of money, in a very short span of time yet make a very strong market presence that will create the foundation for your growth.

If you are using no code AI tools to create your app, then chances are low that you will waste money here. But the real problem will start once you introduce an advanced feature in your app which requires custom coding.

In that case, make sure you aren't stuck in the "development" & "bug fix" loop for a long period of time. Keep your app simple instead!

Regardless, using no code AI tool can also waste your time if you are fully stuck in the "creating" new feature phase. Don't do this unless you know your app needs this feature.

Mistake 3: You Feel Good Making This Mistake & Wonder Why No Result Is There Yet.

The mistake 3 is "**Hiring a UI designer who hardly does any UX process**"

This mistake is very similar to mistake #2, however, there is one very serious problem with this mistake. Most of the new founders want to "hire a UI designer" who will deliver a world class look to the site or app they are trying to build. Also, doing UI involves lots of planning and that way, they have a solid roadmap for development, founders think.

That's the problem with this mistake. In the founders' mind, they know they are doing the right job.

Tell you what, currently, the market is filled with fascinating AI tools, Templates, Design Libraries for UI designers.

Even a 6 months experienced UI designer will be able to generate a world class looking App & Website. Which will probably give you a false idea of "you are on the right track". **Pardon me for being too blunt but it is what it is.**

This problem is even more serious because of this "False World Class" look. Neither you can figure out what's wrong nor the visitors. Well, current markets have everything readily available for the designers, developers or even founders who build on their own needs.

Each and every bit of codes for the features are found online, for free.

Each and every design element of that "unique new feature" you are excited about is already available for your UI designer to take and blend it with your brand's theme. The current market has everything except "originality".

"No, my developers' code is 100% original" & "My UI designer made everything from scratch" you may say.

Well, that was not the point. I honestly don't care if any code or design elements are found online or if they use AI tools to generate them. In fact, that would be smart of them if they did. There is a saying that goes like this, "The next generation developers will not be those who write codes. They will be using AI tools to write codes for them. They will have the smartness to properly add those codes to the right place and make perfect adjustments".

And I am all up for that. I, in fact, love that concept.

What I am trying to say is, "developing" or "designing" anything is not hard.

The market has every tool at your disposal to "design" & "develop" that.

So, when your app or website looks world class, it honestly means nothing. We are not talking about "looks" here.

We have to make it "feel" world class. That's a completely different game.

So, coming back, why Hiring a UI designer who hardly does any UX process is a mistake? How can it be avoided? What troubles does it trigger?

1. If the job of the UI designer you hired is only to make the app or site look better, this is very much risky if you have an existing business with existing users. The new design may not interest your previous users even if it is improved.

On the other hand, If you have just started and launched a new app/site, then doing UI without doing UX research may give you a false idea of "doing good". You may get a high number of installs or visits but not a good number of sustainable users.

2. Most of the UI designers will spend hours building "Design library" which is a collection of all the UI elements used in your site. It helps the developers and keeps your product organised. However, it makes no sense if your app/site does not offer any good experience and can not connect with its visitors. The problem is, the UI designer is not responsible for that.

Let me give you an example: Suppose, you have a boat. It has a hole in the bottom. If you keep adding new utilities, such as, new engine, new saddle etc and build some seating arrangements for you to have a party with your friends, it doesn't matter. The boat will sink. You are spending time in a sinking boat.

Hiring a UI designer whose responsibility is to only work on the "looks" is just like investing in a sinking boat.

3. Oftentimes, UI designers create developer-expensive designs which do not add much value to the target visitors/users/customers but takes a lot of time for a developer to put it in code. That means more time & money spent before launching. This type of updates are good when you have a running app/site with money generating users but very fatal when you just launched. Another "investing in sinking boat" scenario.

My friend, I hope you've got an idea already why all the three mistakes are actually creating all those micro problems in your existing or new app/site.

If you are an existing business owner, you should already be able to relate most of the daily activities with what I just mentioned.

The problem is, it takes years to figure out that, - all those micro-issues, repeated launching, customers not coming back and heavy development (& design too) costs are happening only for the 3 reasons. I learned those the hard way. I hope you do not have to do that.

Good news is, if you can solve the 3 mistakes, you can literally solve 90% (or more) of your problems. This is where the

"Addictive Experience" (as shared in the third chapters) comes into play.

Just imagine, no more spending too much time into developers, no more unnecessary investment into UI designers, no more code heavy, time & money expensive app launches and best of all, with minimum spending, you will have a good number of app/site users who will love your app and they will come back again and again. Also, you are growing, everyday.

Let's talk about how we can do that. Let the magic begin!

....

Note: The interesting content of this book actually starts from the next chapter. Take a break if you want, before going to the next chapter. I request your full attention!

Because, like you, I am also very excited!

CHAPTER 2

3 Unconscious Triggers Your Visitors Don't Know They Crave.

The essential difference between emotion and reason is that emotion leads to action, while reason leads to conclusions. - ***Donald B Calne (Neurologist)***

Welcome to the second chapter of this book. At this stage, you realised the importance of UX. You understood that, in the early steps, we should give more attention to UX or User experience processes.

(Founders with an existing website or app published, the importance of UX processes is actually multiplied as you have more potential to gain more users.)

You understand the 3 mistakes from the previous chapter, but you still have doubt, how UX can actually solve those, to be exact, you understand the importance of UX but you are still not sure how it can help your app or website get more visitors or signups or downloads or orders or any other desired actions? Or all?

Am I right in guessing that?

If you have those questions, that means, you are on the right track.

This book is written in this way. This book itself is also written applying the same principles. The "user" of this book is "You".

I made sure, your journey is amazing. I also made sure I trigger your deepest emotions that make you interested in reading this book. You are a perfect example, that it works. The only tool I used here to make you interested is - "Word". Don't get hurt please. I am being very open here because I know my intention is good. That intention is "I don't want you to do the same mistakes I did in my early startup life".

But hold on. Have you got what I just shared? (only a few seconds ago?)... Let me share this again: " The only tool I used here to make you interested is words".

Just imagine, if only simple words can make a person like you take action (which is to continue reading this book), what would happen if we could have the freedom to add colors, forms, buttons, images, videos, interactions, sounds and most importantly the freedom to add anything we want?

Exactly! The power your app and website have over your visitors is insanely huge. How sad it is to witness founders (& designers), not realising the power they have, keep spending countless hours & money trying to "improve" the app and website which result in almost nothing!

This chapter is your first step to understanding your power and how you can leverage those. All the top tech companies know this and this is how they design & build their app.

I am going to share all those secrets with you.

In this chapter we are going to go deep and understand the **deepest psychology behind our actions.** Especially what triggers us to take actions, i.e. the art of why we do what we do.

Let's start with talking about a part of our body that we use in every activity of our life, but hardly we realize that we are using this.

Let's get introduced to our brain. (Disclaimer: I do not hold any official degree in neuroscience, nor have I studied it vastly. But I had curiosity and I researched on this topic just like any normal person would do.)

Our brain is a very huge complex part of our body. It has billions of nerve cells called neurons. The neurons communicate with each other by sending electronic signals from one neuron to another with the help of neurotransmitters. The electric signal can also be called "messages" in laymen's terms.

This "message" influences our body, thoughts and other perceptions. We become sleepy, hungry, excited, motivated based on the content of the message.

Human behaviour and emotions are hugely complex processes and for such complex behaviours, scientists are trying to find patterns responsible for brain activity with the actions that we take. This is immensely huge and scientists are still trying to figure it out and they have done a good job on it because now we can confidently say we know what part of our brain is responsible for what action.

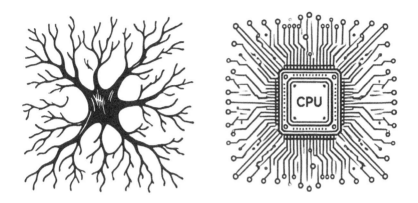

Fig 2.1: Neural Network & Computer's CPU

So this is what we know:

1. The brain has billions of Neurons which together build an immensely huge network. Neurons use neurotransmitters to send messages or electric signals from one part of the brain to another or to our body. The type of message the neurons are sending are responsible for our current state.

2. It controls our hunger, thirst, vision, motor actions, emotions, sensations and regulates our bodily activities. It actually controls every activity that we are aware and unaware of.

3. We are not aware of the activities happening within our brain in normal consciousness.

4. But we are aware of our actions & senses.

5. When we are happy, our brain releases a certain kind of neurotransmitter and some parts of the brain start showing activity. When we are sad, certain parts of the brain show activity.

   (If you feel bored reading about brains, I urge you to keep reading, it's important!)

6. We process information through our senses. The brain compiles that information. Based on that information, the brain sends signals to its other parts. It also sends messages to the body which triggers action.

7. That means, Step 1: Information, Step 2: Brain Compilation, Step 3: Brain sending messages to body, Step 4: Action. Information humans consume has the power to change their actions.

8. Without us even knowing, every information we see, touch, sense are passed through the brain, by triggering, firing some specific parts of the brain resulting in some specific emotions that send some very specific signals to the body part which is a signature of that specific information triggering very specific part of our body which result into action. All those happen without us noticing the processes.

9. If we want people to take the actions, we have to supply them with the information which while being processed by the brain triggers a specific set of emotions we want them to feel which triggers them to take those actions.

10. Point number #9 is important for our cause. If you want, read it again.

11. Point #9 is important for every professional. Salesmen, musicians, producers, marketers and basically every human being, if they want other people to buy their products, listen to their musics, love their movies, etc can use point #9.

12. Point #9 is a science available for anyone to use.

13. We have to figure out our way to use this science for our cause.

14. Read #13 again.

In a very few sentences, what I just shared should make you millions of dollars in the future. Yes, you have to put in the effort and do the hard work, but this information is pure gold!

If you still don't comprehend the importance of this information, let me try by sharing the step by step processes which happen with every one of us:

Step 1: We see information.

Step 2: That information is processed by our brain.

Step 3: The brain generates "messages".

Step 4: We take action based on that unique message.

So, if your goal is "more signups", "more sales", you need to supply information or "experience" from your app that makes the visitors' brains generate messages that make them take the desired action.

Hence, the information or visual experience your app supplies
should not focus on making it look unique, rather the focus should
be to generate enough spark in the visitors' brains that generates
enough messages within their system that they take that desired
action (which is, as I've already said, signup/download/order or
any other action)

Let's talk about how we can do that.

You need to know the 3 unconscious triggers which not only you
visitors but everyone craves.

Let's talk about those one by one from the next sections of this
chapter.

Trigger 1: Happiness In Action

Let's talk about Dopamine.

For those who don't know yet and are thinking "What is Dopamine?" - It is a type of neurotransmitter which is released by the brain's hypothalamus.

Scientists have found that Dopamine is mostly responsible for our happiness. When you feel good, achieve something, eat nice food and win a game etc. more dopamine is released in your brain and your happiness level increases. With that, comes motivation, focus and desire to take action that generates more dopamine.

Dopamine is responsible for our motivation, desire, reward system, happiness and curiosity.

Drinking alcohol and using illegal drugs also release dopamine resulting in making people more happy. No wonder, people get addicted to using illegal drugs because of the happy feelings they get as a result of more dopamine release in their brain.

After their happy period is over, they want to feel the same feelings they felt previously and take those drugs again and again. That's how they get addicted.

Now almost every high school student, coach, and founder knows about the Dopamine effect and how it is responsible for our happiness, addiction and also diseases.

Here is a secret that top tech companies do in their websites and apps. They design their app & website in such a way that is wired to the visitors' reward getting mechanism that releases more dopamine in their visitors' mind and as a result of that, visitors become more happy.

When your brain releases more dopamine, you don't realise it or feel it. Like many unconscious things that happen in your brain, this too is unconscious. However, this secret is applied in every arena in life.

Every marketer designs their marketing ads in such a way that triggers Dopamine in their target customers' mind when they see the ad. "Make your friends surprised by looking sexy" - and then an image of a slim girl with a smiling face and people around the girl look shocked by seeing this beautiful pretty slim girl. Then the "Order now today to get 50% discount" text with a cell phone number. Talking about an ad of a herbal tea that is subconsciously triggering the reward mechanism system of women who are insecure about their weight.

Every restaurant designs their restaurant experience in such a way that makes you crave the food more. Red color (reminds us about hunger), smoky food image (creates saliva) and of course buy 1 and get 1 free with a spontaneous image of a young group of high school students having a very good time triggers you into thinking, if you come to this restaurant, you are also going to have a good time here. Again, targeting for your dopamine.

Netflix shows you all that information in each movie that triggers your brain into releasing more dopamine. The "personal match" rating gives you an idea of personal experience, again saying "You will like this". Then it will show you the "Because you watched this" section that shows you a list of similar shows, trying to remind you "remember the last movie you watched? How happy were you when you watched that?"

Not to mention all those thumbnails with short dressed sexy & handsome men & women, making you think about "sex", again targeting your dopamine.

Facebook, Tiktok, Instagram etc are like modern TVs. You can keep scrolling your whole life being curious "what's next" and before you exit from the app, another new post or story or reels will come beg your attention and you will stay a little longer because "okay, this might be interesting" and before you get bored and close it down, another new reel will come with a 10 seconds renewable expiry date.

All the top tech companies know these secrets. It's nothing new. It has been happening since the dawn of time lol.

That's not all. Another very interesting neurotransmitter is widely used to hook consumers. Let's go to the next section of the chapter.

Trigger 2: Trust In Action

Serotonin is another very important neurotransmitter that is also responsible for our happiness (just like Dopamine). Also it is tied with trust, respect and social bonding. That's why Serotonin is also called the "Social" hormone.

Both Serotonin and Dopamine make us happy but they have different agendas. If Dopamine makes us happy through goal setting, receiving a price, eating food etc. then Serotonin makes us happy by being a part of a community, making new friends, following what our friends and families are doing, helping others, being kind, doing selfless activities, loving others etc.

When you are seeing websites showing you social proof of their products, such as testimonials, videos of "How to use" by real people, they are targeting your Serotonin.

When you have a good amount of Serotonin released in your body, you become trustworthy and you tend to trust others as well.

Netflix does that by showing "No #1 watched movie in your country" title by letting you know that other people in your country are watching this movie. Inside of your brain, you will feel more trust towards that particular movie because your brain is releasing Serotonin already, without you even knowing it is happening.

In various websites, you may have noticed, they are showing their partner fortune 500 companies or big clients they are working with. It's actually for you to have more trust in their brand, again targeting your Serotonin.

When you feel more trust, you become less rational and your chance of taking their service or buying products from them increases.

Here are few important points about when you have Serotonin in your system:

1. It makes you calm.
2. You ask less questions. You trust more.
3. You want to share more.
4. You want to be a part of the bigger group or community.
5. You become kinder.
6. Overall improvement in your moods is observed.

We can use this science in our website/app designing to make our visitors' trust our service more.

Oftentimes, in ecommerce websites, buyers leave the website at the checkout page because they couldn't completely trust the website or the product they wanted to purchase.

For your SAAS app/website or if your app provides any benefit to your visitors and it requires your visitors to put their credit card information to get the benefit, your visitors may leave your site at once if the "trust" part is not fulfilled.

Triggering Serotonin with testimonials, partnership logo, feedback ratings etc. can boost visitors' Serotonin level and help you with incomplete transactions.

Before we discuss in detail about creating addictive UX for your app/website, it is important you have some theoretical understanding of those neurotransmitters.

In the next section, I'll share the third important neurotransmitter needed for our cause.

Trigger 3: The Visitor Who Is Relaxed

Endorphins are another important neurotransmitter. It is responsible for pleasure. It is also called "Natural pain killer". It reduces your pain, boosts self esteem and makes you confident.

Doing exercise, having fun, laughing, having sex etc. cause your brain to secrete endorphins and make you happy.

When you learn something, your brain releases Endorphin and you feel good about it. Have you seen in most of the modern apps, in the loading screen, instead of showing the loading icon, they share "Quotes" of famous people?

This is a good example of giving you information to learn thus making you happy and if you learn that information, your brain will trigger Endorphin making you more calm and relaxed.

What a great idea! The app is making you stress free and calm before showing you their offers/activities.

By providing users with something to learn or ponder, even during moments of downtime, apps are tapping into a psychological trigger that makes users feel good and more connected to the experience. It's a win-win—users get a break from the traditional loading screen, and their brain rewards them for the mental engagement.

This also sets the stage for the app to present its content or offerings in a more positive, open-minded state, as the user is already in a relaxed, endorphin-boosted mood.

The question is,

"Okay, understood. But how can we create the App/Website in such a way that triggers all those neurotransmitters?"

Good question. I am sure you can already guess that we are going to apply neuroscience in our UX processes so that when we design the experience (& interface) of a digital product, we can make it in such a way that it helps the visitors to be happy, calm and motivated.

We will talk about the whole process in the next chapter called "Creating Addictive User Experience". It does not matter who your customers/target users are or what industry you operate in. This formula can help you figure out what your target users crave &

give you actionable steps to implement that either by yourself, or with your UI & UX designer or Product Designer. No matter how unique your situation is.

Second question, "Will this theory or strategy work for every kind of website or app and on every type of user?"

Answer: Yes and absolutely yes.

But here's the thing, What may work for you may not work for your friends.

Let me give you an example: Suppose, you are a basketball player. You are outgoing and you love to go out and have some sort of activities with your friends. You have one friend who is not that outgoing and does not enjoy playing basketball. Even though both of you are good friends, you have different programming for dopamine release.

When you hear the word "basketball" or watch a basketball game or are presented with the possibility of playing basketball with your friends the next day, your brain triggers Dopamine inside.

On the other hand, Dopamine will not get triggered for your friend when presented with the idea of basketball playing. For your friend, the idea of watching a movie together may release Dopamine.

In order for us to get benefits of this strategy, we will have to divide our target users in different groups based on their common hobbies, interests and personalities. We'll have to then match the most common element and then apply it into our strategy. We will talk more about this in the next chapters.

Third question, "Is it manipulation"?

Answer: No. First of all, this book is not about morality and ethics. This book is also not about how to be a good human being (or bad). This book is about how we can make our visitors addicted to our web/app.

The term "addicted" portrays a negative image in our mind. However, see, everyone is addicted to something, good or bad. I am personally addicted to tea.

I am also addicted to some of my favourite places from my childhood. I am addicted to product designing and I am so addicted to this that I am even writing a book. I don't mind being addicted to all this.

What I am trying to say is, your visitors are also normal human beings and regardless of good & bad they are addicted to something already. And I am a firm believer that, if you can't make your visitors stay longer at your site or app, that's your discredit. Someone else will do it and will take away your visitors.

In short, no this is not manipulation. But if your customers/visitors don't get what they want, they are not gonna stay no matter how hard you try to entice them, therefore, eventually they are gonna leave or uninstall.

If they get what they expected, then you are actually doing a service to your visitors. Besides giving them what they need, you are making them happy, motivated & stress free. Your competitors are not offering such experience. Your visitors are not getting the experience you are offering from anywhere else, that's how you become unique.

That's how you create a long-term loyal userbase. Once your visitors use your service/app/website for a long time, it becomes part of their habit. They become repeat users, they share your app/website and your app/website becomes #1 in your niche.

Now, it's time for us to learn about creating "Addictive User Experience" in your app or website in any niche from any industry with any type of target customer or user no matter what your app/website idea is.

Let's go

Chapter 3

Creating Addictive User Experience

Your customers don't care about your product. They care about themselves. - ***Joe Pullizzi (Epic Content Marketing)***

Ah! I had to wait for a long time to come to this chapter. Well done! You've reached halfway in your journey of creating an addictive user experience. Now you know the 3 mistakes to avoid, that means you are more alert and conscious in making your app decisions. You are also with good energy to take care of difficult tasks at ease.

All the previous chapters were helpful in establishing the foundation for you to understand the fact that, "we unknowingly, crop out the UX Research part in our early processes without realising how powerful UX research can be in terms of our app or website business's future".

Let's just clarify what we have understood so far, to be sure that we all are on the same page:

- Offering unique "features" in your website/app is not enough. You need to offer a unique "experience". To provide "unique experience", you need to create an "experience" that your visitors "crave". Only then, your visitors/users will come back, stay longer, do transactions or signups, and start subscribing to your app/service.

- UX research is actually very easy and founders should be part of that. In this chapter we will talk greatly about that.

- Most of the founders (as I did in my first 4 years of business) waste time & money by hiring developers & UI designers before doing proper UX research and not knowing what customers want.

- Proper UX research reveals how the product should look like. It removes unnecessary meetings, brainstorming sessions in the early processes while saving development cost and time. It also reveals what features founders need to focus first.

- All the top companies do UX research and the blending of Neuroscience in the UX process is an open secret. But the press & media prefers to give all the credits to "Market Research" only. Since the term "UX research" is not being mentioned, it remains in the shadows and only a few people understand this.

- UX Research is not an exclusive domain for tech companies only. Every company (from automotive to real estate, from clothing to food, from healthcare to agriculture industry) does that, with different names.

- You can apply these principles to attract visitors to your app/site. But what you promise to offer should be delivered. Otherwise, it becomes manipulation and no long term benefit can be achieved from it.

Now let's jump into the heart of the secret. "How can we build an addictive experience?"

Well, creating an "Addicting User Experience" requires a combination of 3 parts:

- First, it needs to be designed for the **right user group**.
- Second, you should find what **emotionally triggers** that right user group.
- Third, the triggers you find for that user group should be placed in the **right place of the app.**

Just like a tree has 3 parts: i) Root, ii) Trunk and iii) Branches, creating addictive user experience is also a combination of those 3 parts.

We can call this, The Tree of Creating Addicting User Experience (Fig 3.1).

Understanding the 3 parts is crucial, although it may look very simple.

Why is it crucial?

1. Because, if you fail to find the right user group, it doesn't matter if you find the emotional triggers and place those in your digital product. Just like a tree. If you cut the roots, the tree dies.

Trigger Placement (Branches)

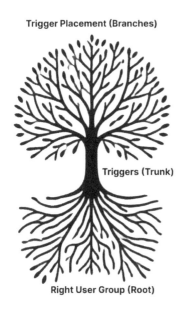

Triggers (Trunk)

Right User Group (Root)

2. On the other hand, let's say, you've found the right user group (root). That means nothing unless you find the triggers for them and put them in the right place in your app/website.

Fig 3.1: The Tree of Creating
     Addicting UX

3. Finally, even if you find the right user group and find the emotional triggers, those will only bring results if you successfully place those triggers to the **right** place of the app or website.

Doing these 3 processes is hard but not impossible.

You have to agree to do the hard & boring work here. I emphasize and invite you to do this because even though it is a hard path, it's not harder than wasting countless hours and money for nothing.

In the end, it's worth doing the hard work to do this task properly. Regarding this, I can share some wisdom with you before going to the next chapter,

"The hard way is the easy way".

The Root: Find the Right User Group

Let's begin talking about the first step to build an addictive user experience that results in more signups, downloads, orders or any desired action you want your visitors/users to take in your website or app.

In the field of business, finding the right user group has always been the key and a crucial step. Therefore, readers from all stages of their business journeys, should carefully read and study this chapter!

Let's imagine, you are building an app that lets people rent bicycles and you want to build an addictive experience in the app. The first step you have to take is to find the "right user group" for this app.

There is a saying that goes, "If you are building for everyone, you are actually building for none". The meaning of this quote is very straight forward. If you are targeting everyone, you will be serving nobody.

So, for your bicycle renting app, first you have to figure out a specific group of people. If you say "everyone", you are not going to be able to create an addictive experience.

"But Mahir, if that is the case, how can I make more profit in the long run?. I want to sell to a lot of people" you may say.

Well, here is the answer "You don't have to stick to only one group of users for your whole life. It's only for the beginning. Once you start with one specific group of users and find success, then you can find another group of users and create features for them and then keep going".

But always remember to start with only one right group of users!

You may start processing more questions now in your head, like "but that will be too late then", "how can I convince investors then?" etc etc.

I promise, I will answer all of your questions and will clear all of your confusions. Just keep reading for now :).

First, create a list of potential user groups for your bicycle renting app. The list can be like this:

1. High School Students
2. Deliverymen
3. Athletes

4. University Students
5. Organisations having large warehouses
6. Professionals (Like doctors, lawyers, teachers who go out everyday to work)

The list can be very big. But for our case, let's stick to 6 user groups only. Among the 6 user groups, our job is to find "one" "right" user group.

That means, not only we'll have to find one user group, we'll have to make sure that the user group is "right" for us.

In order to know which user group is "right" for us, we have to get more information from the list of 6 user groups:

1. What is the total number of people in each group?
2. How easy it is for us to reach each group?

Please note: The "Addictive User Experience" can be applied when you work with only 1 group of users in the beginning. It still can be applied to more than one or two types of groups. But the more groups you merge, the less addiction triggers we can place. This is why it is best to start with one user group first. Then slowly go to 2nd, 3rd, 4th, 5th and so on. It may look like you are slowing down, but actually this helps you grow faster.

Also, please note: it is not the job of the UI&UX designers or product designers to decide the target user group for you, it's your job. Yes, they may be involved in the process and they may suggest to you who should be the "right" group of users, but eventually it falls on you as the founder to find the right user group. For bigger companies, it depends on many factors, such as your business model, product type, strategic relationship you have with other companies and research data from the marketing team.

I merely gave you two metrics to decide your primary target user but you may have more preferences and your business may require more metrics such as: existing relationship (maybe you are already in business with organisations having large warehouses, therefore reaching out to them is not difficult for you), ease to serve (maybe some user groups is easy to serve) etc.

Anyways, back to the point.

Let's say, after you have figured out the size and the ease of reachability, this is how the list looks:

(For the "ease of reachability" just give a score from 1 to 3, 1 being the hardest and 3 being the easiest to reach.)

User Group	Size	Ease of Reachability
High School Students	86K	2
Deliverymen	5K	1
Athletes	6.5K	1
University Students	10K	2
Organisations having large warehouse	100	2
Professionals (Like Bankers, Healthcare	30K	3

workers, Executives etc.)		

For the ease of reachability, say, from research you've concluded that, high school students may already have bicycles and they may not be interested in the "renting" concept as most of the high school students already have their own bicycle. But some students may still be interested, this is why the score is 2.

On the other hand, deliverymen may not be interested in renting bicycles as it may be expensive for them. Also, most of the deliverymen may already have bicycles or cars. Therefore, reaching them might be very difficult. Therefore the score is 1.

An athlete may also not be interested in the "renting" concept. Therefore the score is 1.

Hope you've got the idea. So I am skipping the next two user groups to save time to talk about the final group "Professionals".

Let's say, we've discovered that most of the professionals go to their workplace by public transportation and they waste their travel time by waiting in traffic as most of their workplaces are in the busier side of the city.

Let's say, we've also found that most of the professionals are also concerned about their growing belly fat which they can't control due to lack of exercise.

It seemed like a good idea, to offer them "bicycle renting" service which they can utilize during their daily commute to work while it also involves physical movements which has a potential to reduce belly fat. Therefore, we gave this user group a score of "3".

From the above list, it looks like the "Professionals" user group is the "right" user group for our "Bike Rental" app as they are fairly good in number of size (which is 30K) and also it would be easy to convince them to use our "Bike rental" app service.

(Please note: The scenario may be entirely different in real life, but my objective here is to just share the underlying thought process to choose your "one" "right" user group to build an addictive user experience so that your app or website service can get more signups or any desired action(s).)

In our hypothetical example let's say, key information we found:

- 65% of professionals (that means 19.5K) are not getting enough time to have exercise.
- 15% (that means 4.5K) are very much interested in doing exercise but they don't have any time for that. They can't also do exercise on the weekends because they spend their time with their family.
- Almost 73% of the professionals don't have their own bicycle or they are not interested in buying one.

The list of information can keep going.

Therefore, the group "Professionals" seemed more promising data-wise.

What I just shared is a very easy & basic approach to determine the "right" user group. There is a better approach though. That approach is little bit complex and if I dive into sharing each piece of details for that approach, the book will be unnecessarily lengthy and may deviate the ideal readers of this book from the main objective of this book, which is to "build an addictive experience that results in more signups, more downloads, more orders, more actions etc."

Also, I am assuming that most of you already have one "right" user group determined for your app / website business. If you do not have one, the previous process should give you some idea on how you can find "one" for you.

However, if you are insistent about learning the "better approach" in determining the "right" user group, I have shared the key processes (leaving out the tiny details) in the bonus chapter of this book, so at-least you know the processes and do the rest from your founder level situation. (You can read that after finishing the book.)

Remember, finding the "right" user group is key, so if you are hesitant about the easy approach, I recommend you read the bonus chapter and apply that.

A wrong user group may literally destroy your venture and feed you with wrong input which may cause more loss.

But if you already have found one right user group, no worries then.

You are ready to go to the next chapter.

Discover Emotional Triggers to Hook Them

Now that we've determined and found our right user group, our next job is to discover triggers which are emotionally engaging to that user group.

First let's understand what is a "Trigger"? (Ah! this chapter is gold)

We use this word when using tools, guns, machines etc. Trigger is actually a switch that starts a process.

Suppose, you have come home from work. Your brain needs rest now. You lied down on the bed and idly opened your facebook or instagram or tiktok and started scrolling with no objective.

Your mind wants to be absent from any current work now. We can call this state "Absent state".

In your absent state of internet browsing, you come across a video which you found interesting. You clicked on the video to watch.

After a few seconds, an ad started playing, interrupting your video watching experience.

You became disturbed and you pressed back to get back to your newsfeed not being interested to watch the video anymore. That "ad" triggered your emotions. You became a little bit agitated. Going back to the newsfeed solved your problem.

Then you saw another video with an interesting topic but this time you became very excited because the topic of the video was very exciting for you.

In that video, a CEO was explaining how to get the first 1 million users in your app/site.

That literally hooked you. Time froze, you forgot your thoughts, your focus became 100% active. Suddenly, a rush of vibration started from your head to heart to your whole body. You changed your posture so that you can become more alert and watch this video mindfully.

If you were lying previously, you are now sitting up.

After a few seconds of watching the video which made you super excited, an ad started.

But this time, you did not go back to the newsfeed or home, rather you eagerly waited for the "Skip" button to appear so that you could skip the "ad" and watch the full video.

Why is it different this time?

Because you became very eager to learn what the guy had to say. We can safely say that the video successfully triggered your action which made you more alert, awake and focused.

Neurology-wise, what happened is, first, billions of photons reached your eyes and your eyes sent those information to your brain.

Your brain, while processing that information, realised, the information is related to your passion.

Your brain is probably the world's most amazingly functioning accurate "pattern recognition system" which can immediately know which information matches with your desires, goals, plans and what part of your emotions or past experiences.

So, it knows that you are interested in your app business and this video is talking about exactly that. It triggered dopamine.

You felt the rush. You became motivated. Your brain sent enough electricity to your body that triggered you to take action, which was, to "watch the video".

Another interesting thing happened here. That is "Anticipation". The topic of that particular video itself created an anticipation which triggered the reward system of your brain.

Unconsciously, you thought, "okay, this video will help me get my first 1 million users". Even an ad couldn't interrupt you, which didn't happen with the first example.

A very important thing to note here: What your visitors experience must be more interesting and hooking than outside distractions/ad popups etc.

Now let's talk about our goal.

Your app/site shouldn't be like the first video where you pressed the back button as soon as an ad started. This is where most of the site/app loses in business. You don't want to be the first video. You want to be the second video.

To be more precise, your app should be like the second video.

Wait Mahir, you were talking about apps/sites, how come now you are giving references to videos?

(Fig 3.2: A user is triggered by a content. Can your app do that?)

Good question, I tried to give you an easy example which happens with your day to day life.

The video example seemed a good analogy to me to give you how it feels to get hooked.

But you have to understand, the concept is the same for your app/website too.

You have to make your visitors hooked whether it is a video or an app or a website or even a restaurant. This situation is the same for scenarios..

Wouldn't that be amazing, if your visitors who are exploring/browsing or using your app or site feel the same way that you just felt? When even outside distractions, ads can't take away your visitors?

That is our goal.

If you can just do that for one person in your target user group, you can do that for many people from the same group. Because most of the characteristics will match as they belong to the same group. **That's why choosing one primary group is essential.**

Our job for this chapter is to gather as many triggering points as we can that generate dopamine, endorphin & serotonin in our visitors' brain and use those triggering points in our app/site.

Simple!

Here is a list that contains some fundamental motivation factors which triggers those productive hormones to almost any human's brain:

1. Food.
2. Sex.
3. Money.
4. Reward/Achievement.
5. Learning.
6. Travelling.
7. Doing favourite activities/hobbies etc.
8. Socialising/making new friends/meeting new people etc.
9. Being kind, helping others.
10. Love.
11. Being a good parent/ good human being.
12. Receiving compliments from others.
13. Getting recognition.
14. Achieving goals / accomplishing a task.
15. Surprise.

and also many many more factors.

One pro tip: "Anticipation" of any of the above items works multiple times better. We'll talk about this in detail.

For our bicycle renting app, if we want to build an addictive experience, we need to find the emotional triggers for the user group (Professionals).

Discovering emotional trigger is a two step process:

1. Craft a deep user persona from surveys.
2. Discover emotional desires & frustrations from having a direct interview.

Step 1: Craft a deep user persona from surveys.

In order to find triggers, typically, UI & UX designers create "user personas" by doing research and interviews. In most cases, typical user personas don't help us create an experience that attracts the target visitors let alone hook them and keep them coming back again and again.

In most user personas, founders, UI&UX designers like to add age, profession, favourite hobby, activities, frustration, problems, motivations etc.

I also did that for many years until I realised that, actually the core reason we build user persona is to understand the **psychology of the user group.**

I realised, the typical user persona model is not enough. It is okay but we should dive deep and improve the typical User Persona the industry uses.

Therefore, I would like to construct an updated version of the user persona. I like to call it, "Deep User Persona".

Generating the "Deep User Persona" is going to answer all the questions we need. It's a simple process and it's very fun.

Let's create a "Deep User Persona" for our target user group - the "Professionals".

It is ideal, we set up both an interview session with them and also run a survey. I emphasize on doing both because, when we are doing an interview, we have the chance to observe them, discover where they pause, where they emphasize and gain more insights on their emotions.

On the other hand, I like to do surveys, because "surveys" are passive and give us some insights which are hard to find in direct interviews. Our target users have to fill it up digitally, by writing with keyboards or clicking on multiple choice options. While filling up the survey form, their responses might be different than having direct interview sessions resulting in more opportunities for us to learn.

So, the best path is to do both.

Let's create a sample survey form for our target user group "Professionals".

Create a survey form

(From below, the survey form starts)

— — — — —

Welcome!

Thank you for taking a moment to help us design a better commuting experience for busy professionals like you. Your feedback will help us create an app that combines exercise and convenience, empowering you to make your daily commute healthier, more sustainable, and stress-free!

Your Privacy Matters

We value your trust. All the information you share in this survey will remain strictly confidential and will only be used to improve our services. No personal data will be shared with third parties.

1. **How do you currently commute to work?**
   - ○ A) Public transport
   - ○ B) Car
   - ○ C) Walking
   - ○ D) Bicycle

2. **How long does your daily commute usually take?**
   - ○ A) Less than 15 minutes
   - ○ B) 15–30 minutes
   - ○ C) 30–60 minutes
   - ○ D) More than 1 hour

3. **Do you currently exercise during your daily routine?**
   - ○ A) Yes, regularly
   - ○ B) Sometimes

○ C) Rarely

○ D) No, not at all

4. **What is your biggest challenge with commuting?**

○ A) Traffic and delays

○ B) No challenge

○ C) Cost of transportation

○ D) Stress or lack of convenience

5. **What motivates you most to stay active?**

○ A) Improving physical health

○ B) Reducing stress

○ C) Saving time

○ D) Environmental impact

6. **How would you describe your lifestyle?**

○ A) Highly active and health-conscious

○ B) Moderately active

○ C) Sedentary, but looking to become more active

○ D) Sedentary with no immediate plans to change

7. **Would you be interested in combining exercise with your commute?**

   ○ A) Definitely

   ○ B) Maybe

   ○ C) Unlikely

   ○ D) Not at all

8. **What type of exercise appeals to you the most?**

   ○ A) Cardiovascular (e.g., cycling, running)

   ○ B) Strength training

   ○ C) Yoga or mindfulness activities

   ○ D) Group or social activities

9. **What would be the most important feature in a bike-rental app?**

   ○ A) No space needed for me to park

   ○ B) Easy booking and access

   ○ C) Safety and reliability

   ○ D) Variety of bike options

10. **What would prevent you from using a bike rental service?**

    ○ A) Cost too high

○ B) Lack of bike lanes or safety concerns

○ C) Not enough rental stations nearby

○ D) Uncertainty about weather conditions

11. What do you value most in your daily routine?

○ A) Efficiency and time management

○ B) Maintaining physical and mental well-being

○ C) Cost-effectiveness and saving money

○ D) Sustainability and eco-friendliness

12. How often do you use apps for fitness, transportation, or productivity?

○ A) Daily

○ B) A few times a week

○ C) Occasionally

○ D) Rarely or never

13. How would you prefer to pay for a bike rental service?

○ A) Pay-per-use

○ B) Weekly subscription

○ C) Monthly subscription

○ D) Part of a larger fitness or commute package

14. What amenities or services would you want near bike rental stations?

○ A) Lockers or secure storage

○ B) Charging stations for devices

○ C) Nearby cafes or relaxation spots

○ D) Maintenance or repair support

15. What kind of bike features are most important to you?

○ A) Comfort and ease of use

○ B) Electric assistance for longer distances

○ C) Safety features (lights, reflectors, etc.)

○ D) Customizable options (e.g., baskets, child seats)

———————

(The survey ends here)

Pro tip: Use ChatGPT to start building the form. Don't fully rely on ChatGPT but use this to fast forward the process. It shouldn't take more than 2 hours of your time to generate the form.

Now the fun part begins.

Send the survey form to 100+ people

Now it's time for you to send this to a group of professionals. You can use an email list or run an Ad. If you don't have any email list, no worries! Run an Ad in Meta, Instagram, Tiktok, Twitter, Linkedin or Google ad for a few days. My preference is 3 days 24 hours. Better to choose only one platform or two platforms at most. For our case, we can use Linked In or Facebook or both.

I am not going to elaborate on how you are going to get responses for this form. You can even go to any corporate event and manage to get plenty of people to fill up the form. You can use a marketing agency to do that for you. I am assuming, one way or the other you will figure that on your own.

Since this book is about how we can make an addictive experience on App/Site, I am going to skip the data collection part. But overall, the easiest is to run ads.

Get the winning answers!

Let's gather the responses and get the winning answers from all the questions. Let's say, this is what we got:

1. How do you currently commute to work? **- B) Car**
2. How long does your daily commute usually take? **- B) 15-30 minutes**
3. Do you currently exercise during your daily routine?**- B) Sometimes**
4. What is your biggest challenge with commuting? **- A) Traffic and delays**
5. What motivates you most to stay active? **- A) Improving physical health**
6. How would you describe your lifestyle? **- B) Moderately active**
7. Would you be interested in combining exercise with your commute? **- C) Unlikely**
8. What type of exercise appeals to you the most? **A) Cardiovascular (e.g., cycling, running)**
9. What would be the most important feature in a bike-rental app? **D) Variety of bike options**
10. What would prevent you from using a bike rental service? **A) Cost too high**

11. What do you value most in your daily routine? - **A) Efficiency and time management**

12. How often do you use apps for fitness, transportation, or productivity? - **C) Occasionally**

13. How would you prefer to pay for a bike rental service? - **A) Pay-per-use**

14. What amenities or services would you want near bike rental stations? - **C) Nearby cafes or relaxation spots**

15. What kind of bike features are most important to you? - **A) Comfort and ease of use**

Congratulations! You are now ready to create "deep user persona"

The above 15 answers are our first step to create a deep user persona for our target users and create an addictive experience for them.

Btw, if you have any confusion regarding how critical & careful we should be in creating the form, for instance, what questions should we ask, what options should we put in the answer section, the answer is, the form doesn't have to be super perfect.

It's just a good practice to make this easy, simple and also engaging but don't try too hard on this.

If you keep an open mind, and just follow the steps, eventually you will reach the final stage. Here, the important part is not doing things "accurately" as there is no "right answer". The importance is to just follow the process, without thinking about right or wrong.

Remember that, you still haven't invested that much. So, money wise, you are good.

An important point to keep in mind is that, always take the winning answer for the question. That's the "Deep User Persona" for the "Professional" group. This part is very important.

Create deep user persona summary

If we look at the winning answers, our deep user persona suggests, s/he drives car, travels 15-30 minutes, sometimes exercises, does not like traffic & delays, want to be active by doing physical exercise, stays moderately active, does not want to combine exercise while commuting, likes cardiovascular exercise like cycling, running etc., likes variety of bike options while renting, does not like too much cost in bike renting, wants to be efficient and time organised, occasionally use fitness app, likes to pay per rent model, wants bike renting stations from cafes, relaxation spots, like comfortable and easy bikes.

Let's now divide all the points into 3 parts: activity, like, dislike

Activity:

- Drives car
- Travels 15-30 minutes
- Sometimes exercise

Like:

- Cardiovascular exercise
- Variety of bike choosing option
- Pay per rent model
- Comfortable and easy bikes
- Physical activity

Dislike:

- Traffic & Delay
- Exercising with commuting
- Too much cost

Apart from any top points, if you still have other points to mention, just put them under "Note". Let's write the "Note" section.

Notes:

Also, this user group wants the bike renting stations to be near to cafes and relaxation spots.

Well done! you are one step ahead in offering the "Addictive User Experience". Let me remind you the happy news, which is, you haven't spent a penny yet in building the app, hurray!. Maybe you spent a few bucks on collecting the data but you were gonna do that anyway.

We have one more step remaining in discovering emotional triggers for our target user group. We now need to have a direct interview session with one or two persons from our target user group. Once that part is done, our "discovering emotional trigger" stage is also done.

Now, let's do a direct interview session with a user.

Step 2: Discover emotional desires & frustrations from having a direct interview session

Find someone from your community who belongs to the definition of our "Professional" group's deep user persona. That means, someone who matches the "winning profile" we discovered in the first step from the survey.

It doesn't matter if you find that person from the survey, close colleagues or from a random incident, but never engage with someone who already knows you, because that way, that person will only tell you what you want to hear.

Below is a detailed transcript of an example interview for a professional group.

Interview Session: John from XYZ Company

John's profile:

John is 35. Currently working at a Marketing Agency as a senior creative executive. He commutes using his own car. It takes around 30-35 minutes for him to reach his office. He wants to have some physical activity but not getting enough time due to work and with his two kids. He likes to travel, hike and likes to spend time with his family.

Interview Place:

Zoom Online Video Conference. Both of the attendants' videos are on. Zoom video recording is also happening.

The Interview Transcript:

Interviewer: Hi John, how are you? My name is Mahir.

John: Hey Mahir, I'm good how's it going?

Interviewer: Good good (smiling). Thank you very much for agreeing to meet me.

John: Sure (smiling). Love to be of help.

Interviewer: (Slow head nodding) So, as you know. I just want some opinion from you regarding an app we are launching. (Pause) Looks like you are totally the person for whom we are building the app and we would love to get some clarity from your side which will help us better design the app.

It's very simple. I will ask you a few questions, all I need is your honest answers (smile).

John: (Head nods). Sure (smiling)

Interviewer: Can you tell me a bit about your professional life?

John: Sure. So, I work at this Marketing Agency where I am the Senior Creative Director. Our company mostly works with clients with luxury brands, mostly perfume brands. (Pause) We run shows from all over Europe and organize fashion shows, exhibitions, press conferences for our clients. I take care of the creative sides such as the arts, exhibits, models etc.

Interviewer: Interesting! You must travel a lot! (Smiling)

John: A lot, I just came from Paris a few days ago. Next month, we are going to Zurich for an inauguration ceremony of a new perfume brand. Already the entire team is working very hard, talking to journalists, influencers and making sure the show is at the top of attraction.

Interviewer: That's amazing! Lucky guy. So what's the plan? What would you like to do in the future? Any goal you are trying to achieve recently?

John: Tricky question! Right now, the only focus is to work. Not much.

(The interviewer realized John was uncomfortable answering the question. So he wanted to help John)

Interviewer: So, our app is designed for professionals like you. With the app, we want to make sure, if there is some common goal we can find. For instance, say, you have a dream of buying a house or travelling or you are saving up for opening your own business or maybe you want to become more fit. That's why I was asking (smiling).

John: Got it. Ya that makes sense. So, I have three goals in my life. I kinda like the bohemian lifestyle. So, I want to retire by the age of 45. I am already saving up and have invested in many different segments. Once I reach (USD) 1 million in my bank account, I will retire. That's one goal. Another one is, I want to travel the whole world with my wife Sarah. I mean, I already traveled a lot. But I want to travel more (smiling), taste different kinds of foods, learn different languages, meet new people etc.

Third goal is, I want to have my own gallery of arts, where I will showcase all pieces of things I created. I want people to visit my gallery and admire my art. Ya that's it. (Smiling)

Interviewer: Wow! I really like your goals. I also have a similar plan of travelling and meeting new people. The app we are planning to build …… (The interviewer couldn't finish. John interrupted)

John: So what's the app you guys are making?

Interviewer: We are still not fully sure how we are going to make it. But it's something related to professionals commuting to work and giving them an option to have physical activity without having them to spend much time.

(The interviewer is skeptical about sharing the app idea fully because first of all, he wants to get an honest opinion from John. He is afraid John may get biased if he learns about the app idea. Secondly, he is open to the fact that he may entirely change the app's idea in the future. So, no point sharing him an app idea which is not validated yet)

John: I see. Is it some sort of handball type toy, where a person can do hand exercise while driving?

Interviewer: Not really. So, we want to launch a bicycle renting service where busy professionals can rent bicycles and use that to commute. That way, professionals don't have to spend money on purchasing a bicycle, making a place for the bicycle in their apartment and not to mention maintaining it. They can use this to commute which actually boosts their strength, stamina, immunity and makes them physically active.

John: Got it. This sounds like a great idea really! I mean, my wife Sarah pursued me many times to join her in the gym. I accompanied her a few times but eventually, couldn't continue. Sounds like this will be a good option.

Interviewer: Glad to hear that. Do you think you will use our service if we launch that?

John: Ya, of course. Why not?. I can already give you one idea. Most of the people using public transportation often lose their patience waiting for the bus to come in, if you can somehow give them the option to rent at that particular moment, it's a great win for you.

Imagine, a person like me waits for the bus to arrive at the bus stand every day. Sometimes, I miss the bus or sometimes the bus arrives late. So, it is normal, frustration grows out of me. So, if I can see the bicycles everyday during my frustrating period, I will try this one day. Once I try this for one time, chances are high I will try it one more time. Eventually, I will become a regular user.

Interviewer: That's a fantastic idea John. We'll definitely do that. Regarding that, can you tell us how difficult or easy it is for you to commute to your work? Are there any frustrating experiences?

John: So, sometimes I take my own car and sometimes I take the bus. Buses almost always take double the time than cars to reach, plus add the time you need to walk to reach the bus station. Therefore, timewise, buses are a very lengthy commute. But they are also cheap. On the other hand, when I take a car, I reach my destination very quickly but parking takes time. I'd say both the options have their pros and cons. But I think people who live near their workplace may be your ideal target customer. If they live far away, they may not be interested in riding the bicycle.

(The Interviewer realised, the topic is changing from John to their app. The situation which he wanted to avoid.)

Interviewer: Excellent insight. Thank you very much. Can you tell me some situations from your work or life which are frustrating to you?

John: Mmm… let me think (Pause)... to be honest. Apart from the work pressure, there is nothing that's bothering me now. But, work pressure is common for everyone right? So other than that, nothing much.

Interviewer: Okay, now some different questions. Can you name the top 5 apps you use on a regular basis?

John: Sure. I use the message app a lot. I use google map a lot too. Instagram is something I use almost everyday. And yah, I use the notes app and some apps from work.

Interviewer: Do you use any app to track your health? Like steps, calories burned etc?

John: That sounds like Sarah, my wife. She uses Apple's health app.

Interviewer: What activities do you do on weekends?

John: Last week, I went to visit my in-laws. This week, the kids wanted to go to the theme park in New Jersey. We may go there, not sure yet. But usually, we eat dinner outside on the weekends or just relax at home.

Interviewer: Great John. We are almost at the end of the interview. I have one last question for you and then, we are good to go.

John: Sure, go ahead (smiling).

Interviewer: What makes you happy? In general?

John: I really like your questions. Having a good time with friends and family always makes me happy. Now that I have two kids, watching them grow, playing with them, and making memories with them is something which makes me happy.

Interviewer: Awesome. Well, I don't have any further questions for you. So, you are at luck now (Giggling).

John: (Giggling) Honestly, I really enjoyed answering the questions man. Let me know if you need to do this again. I would love to do that again.

Interviewer: Thanks John. Have a good day. Take care!

John: Take care.

(The Zoom video call ended)

—--

I hope you've enjoyed the interview session. From the interview, we have to identify the motivation & frustration that possibly other people from the professional group may have.

I've created a table here based on the interview. On the left side, we will put all the motivation and the right side will be the frustration John has. This table will help us build & design triggers.

Motivation	Frustration
Travelling. Having 1 million dollars in a bank account (Saving). Having his own exhibition of arts in a gallery. Spending time with family.	Work pressure Not getting enough time to work out (his wife wants him to spend time in gym)

With the above personalised motivation and frustration lists, we will create & build our triggers.

Before creating triggers for the professional user group, I have to discuss in more details about what constitutes a good trigger? Well, we already know that a good trigger is something that inspires/motivates the target user group to take action.

We've also understood that a trigger makes the visitors hooked with the app/website. But, before we create a trigger, the question that begs our attention is, What constitutes a good trigger?

A trigger must follow this three step lifecycle:

1. Engagement: The beginning point of a trigger is engagement. An audience must stop for a moment encountering a trigger.

2. Emotion: Encountering the trigger, the audience must feel emotion inside. It can be a happy emotion, it can be a sad emotion or it can be a fear as well. It can also be inspirational.

3. Action: A trigger must make the audience take a desirable action.

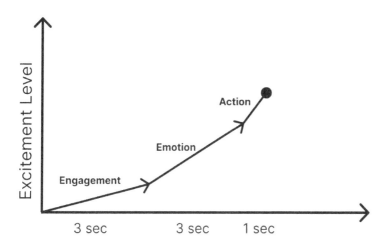

(Fig 3.3: Lifecycle of a trigger)

If you look at the above figure, the horizontal line shows how much time has passed and the vertical line shows the excitement level of the user.

The figure shows us how the excitement level of a user increases as the user goes through a trigger. It also shows that the action stage is the shortest part of a trigger (1 sec). The timeline here is just an example though. Not a fact. Different triggers may have different timelines.

Question, what can constitute a trigger?

So:

1. A trigger can be a text.
2. A trigger can be a video.
3. A trigger can be an image.
4. A trigger can be a button.
5. A trigger can be a combination of text, video, image and button.

If, it can make the audience stop and make them engage, make them feel emotion and make them take action, as shown in the previous figure.

Most of the founders and even designers themselves make this mistake thinking that this concept is only applicable for running facebook or social media ads. Truth is, in your app, you should follow this concept too!

The question is, what does a trigger look like?

Let's see if you can spot any triggers from any real life examples first. Let's check the publicly available apps.

If you search for "Financial App" in the App store, you will find plenty of apps. To show you, I just randomly downloaded a few apps and shared their first screen. Please note that: I am not affiliated with any of the apps nor I don't like or like these apps. Also please note that, to keep things simple, I am only auditing the first screen.

Example 1:

Track Your Expenses

All your spends, bills, credit card, savings and other expenses in one place

Next

(Fig 3.4 App Example 1)

I do not want to address so many UI issues the first screen of this app has because to be honest, when you are adding a new feature or launching a new app, UI matters less than UX.

Let's ask the following questions:

1. Is it making me stop? Answer: Yes, maybe.
2. Is it generating any emotion? Answer: No
3. Is it making me take any action? Answer: Not much.

So this UI is not a trigger. (Note: The image here shows a mom and a child. This can be a good trigger for new moms.)

Example 2:

This app has a better UI than the previous one. But again, does it matter? Not much to be honest!

Let's ask the following questions:

1. Is it making me stop? Answer: Yes, maybe.
2. Is it generating any emotion? Answer: No
3. Is it making me take any action? Answer: Not much.

Also, we're not sure who it is

(Fig 3.5 App Example 2)

for. If it's for general people like you and me, definitely this screen failed to hook us! So this is not a trigger for me or you (I guess), sadly!

(Fig 3.6 App Example 3)

Example 3

This one is offering a very unique UI with somewhat very poor color principles applied. But it doesn't matter to me. I am more interested in checking whether or not it is making me stop & take any action:

Let's ask the following questions:

1. Is it making me stop? Answer: Yes, maybe.
2. Is it generating any emotion? Answer: No
3. Is it making me take

any action? Answer: Not much.

Not sure who this is for. If this is for generic people like you and me, it failed to hook us.

So this UI is not a trigger.

These three are the top finance management apps in the App store when I searched. I can search for hundreds more and still won't find much differences. Some will have some unique features too!

In the coming months, hundreds of new Finance Management apps will be released in the app store with beautiful UI with new unique features powered by new generation AI, only to become an average app that eventually people forget.

Those founders are like my old self. I love them and feel sorry for them at the same time.

Ask them, how much have they spent? Don't get surprised when you hear the answer is between $10K up to $100K or even more.

Well, it isn't that surprising, because behind those poor experiences, trigger-lacking screens, underlying some of the world class features which have been built by world class developers spending countless hours.

Everyone is feature ready. Everyone is UI ready. If you compete with features and UI, you will lose.

Become "experience" ready, you will win the market! by spending less than your competitors.

Question, "Okay, Mahir, understood. Now can you show us what a trigger looks like?"

Yes, of course. Now is the time. Let's say, for our professional group, if we create a personal finance management app, this is how I would design the first screen:

(Please go to the next page)

Look at the screen!

Can you tell the difference?

It's just a simple image and a quote that says "Professionals who manage their financials become millionaire 10 years earlier than professionals who don't"

Let's ask the following questions:

1. Is it making me stop?
   Answer: Yes

(Fig 3.7 Trigger in App)

2. Is it generating any emotion? Answer: Yes.
3. Is it making me take any action? Answer: Yes totally!

This is a very powerful and strong trigger for professionals.

First of all, this screen is directly addressing them and making them stop by using the word "Professionals" at the beginning.

Secondly, look at the image. Most of the Finance Management apps as we have seen before, think that, "Since we are finance management app, we have to show some coins, dollar icon, growth icons etc"

But instead of putting any boring icons, I did the complete opposite. I put a luxury villa image. Because, with research, I found that all the busy professionals have a subconscious underlying dream of having a relaxed time at a luxurious villa or owning one.

Not only that, this newspaper quote also talks about becoming a millionaire which creates "anticipation". The brain's reward getting mechanism is getting activated when a professional reads this. Also the quote kind of gives a suggestion something like "If you manage your money, you will become rich earlier".

(Please note: This news is not real. I made this up just to give you an example. In real life, please do not do this, lol.)

To the professionals, when they open the app and see this first screen, they will immediately get hooked.

The image will generate Dopamine in their internal system that will start making them happy. The Forbes Magazine quote will again generate another dose of Dopamine and Serotonin in their system. Serotonin, as I've mentioned before, is a social hormone.

When our target user group sees the word "Forbes", internally their brain will generate Serotonin. This hormone is also responsible for trust. Hence, the visitor will start trusting the app more. No other apps did offer this experience.

Overall, this UI directly generates dopamine & serotonin in the visitors' brain.

and how much time did I spend designing this screen? Less than 10 minutes to design and say, around 1 hour to research. Also it's not that UI unique. It doesn't look that extraordinary. But does it matter? No!

Because, **to the visitors' eyes, this app will become unique!**

Although, this screen is not fully final yet. I would still want to work on it more. I would like to add the Forbes logo there. Also, I would add a "high-five" icon in the "Start Managing" button. Icons such as high five, love, hug etc also generate serotonin in visitors' brain, research suggests.

Will share about this in the later chapters.

Let me create another design from the previous examples containing triggers.

Among the three examples I've shown you before, the first example had a mother and a child illustration, remember? (Fig 3.4)

I want to show how I would design the first screen for the new mothers. The first example did have a potential if they truly target it for new moms. As a product designer myself, I can't help re-designing or improving something when I find it interesting.

"A financial management app for new mothers" is a very great headline!.

Although I don't have much data on new mothers. I am just gonna use my basic research and want to show you how would I design the first screen:

The image here is the "stopper". It stops the visitors and attracts attention!

The text, by saying "Super mom, financially healthy mom!" creates a feeling of superiority in the moms' minds (provided that the visitor is a new mom).

That superiority in result, generates all those happy hormones within her internal system. Making her trust this app more.

(Fig 3.8 Trigger in a finance app for new mothers)

Mothers usually have an emotional connection with their child. They want to feel "superior" and responsible for their children.

So the superwoman image, followed by the text "Super mom" is a strong trigger for moms, especially the new ones.

Then the call to action button "Start Saving" directly correlates to the idea that, by clicking this button, she will be financially healthy.

Btw, I could have used "financially strong mom!" but I chose "financially healthy mom" because, with my research, I found that "healthy" is a very common word in new moms' dictionary. Instead of "Strong", I've used "healthy" because for new moms, they are always concerned about "health" for themselves and their babies.

Always try to focus on common words of the mind of the audiences'.

I hope you've got an idea on what is a trigger and what is not. To keep things simple, I just used examples of mobile apps. But for websites, the same concept is true.

Just ask yourself, the next time you make a website for your business, does this have any trigger?

If the answer is no, then don't waste time making things beautiful and spending money in developing. Find the triggers first. That's the only secret in this book, that will make you stand out from the crowd, help you generate more signups, more downloads than your competitors and help you spend less in marketing but get better results.

Now hear me out, your app/website must have plenty of triggers. This is actually the main objective of why I am writing this book. Most of the apps and websites found nowadays lack triggers and that is one of the main reasons why visitors are leaving your app or website.

Failing to create "Trigger" means you have not found out the right formula. Customers can't trust you if there is no "Trigger" and eventually your investor will stop supporting you.

Thousands of new founders have amazing ideas, they hire designers or developers and those hired designers or developers follow market ready industry grade world class design that does not generate enough traction, leaving the founders in confusion. Eventually founders learn that the whole approach of the app was wrong, they turn it into a different version of this idea only to learn another costly lesson.

For founders who are already generating revenue and growing, you have no lack of data to research and you are kind of dealing with data mines. Not only that, if you have a marketing team, be sure to know that plenty of data is already existent within the marketing team that can be converted into a series of triggers.

Well, as a founder of a growing team, if your UX team is not collecting / asking for data from the marketing team, they are doing repeat-work and wasting hours.

Now, let's get back to our original topic. Let's build triggers for our professional group for the bike rental app.

Earlier, we discovered the motivation and frustration of one of the persons from the professional group. Oftentime, you may find some motivation or frustration which only belongs to the personal situation of that person. For instance, during the interview, John mentioned his future plan of doing his own exhibition. This is something which is only exclusive to John. For our cause, it means nothing because not all professionals have the same wish. We will omit that.

Now, we are at a good position to create a "Potential Trigger List" for our Professional User Group using the motivation of John (as we've discovered before during the interview with John)

The list of Potential Trigger List for Professional User Group:

1. **(Physical activity)** A trigger that focuses on the physical activity part of the visitor while riding a bicycle. An image showing body parts highlighting muscles can be a hook here. Should have some text that supports the fact.

2. **(Testimonial)** A trigger of a testimonial of a person, who solved a specific problem 'x' by riding a bicycle. Here the quote and the image of the commenter will be the hook.

3. **(Financial benefit)** A trigger of the benefit of riding a bicycle and how it can save fuel costs and help a person achieve his/her saving goal faster. The hook will focus on an image of wealth, money, luxury travel image showing freedom with related text.

4. **(Productivity)** A trigger that shows how riding a bicycle before going to office makes a person productive, smart and how it helps the person generate more creativity in office work. The hook will be an image of the brain, and some research findings that support the statement.

5. **(Stress management)** A trigger that shows how riding a bicycle reduces office stress, elevates mood by making the person happy. The hook can be an image of an office environment where work pressure is too much which is very stressful with a title text that says something about it.

Apart from the top 5 triggers, let's add a few more triggers from our already known motivation which is common for every human being. Remember, the list which I shared with you at the beginning of the chapter? If you can't remember, let me share that list of motivation (which is common for every human being) here again:

1. Sex.
2. Money.
3. Reward/Achievement.
4. Learning.
5. Travelling.
6. Doing favourite activities/hobbies etc.
7. Socialising/making new friends/meeting new people etc.
8. Being kind, helping others.
9. Love.
10. Being a good parent/ good human being.
11. Receiving compliments from others.

12. Getting recognition.

13. Achieving goals / accomplishing a task.

14. Surprise.

In the list, the top 1 is "Sex".

Think, can we incorporate the sex concept with our offering?

Maybe riding a bicycle helps men to perform better in sex? For women, maybe riding a bicycle increases their libido? Need to research on the topic.

Second is money, we've already added this as #3 in the trigger list.

Next is, "learning". Since we are targeting "Professional" people, we can omit this part. It is safe to assume that they already know how to ride a bicycle. Plus, there is nothing much to learn here for them. Same for travelling.

(Please note: If you find this chapter confusing and hard to grasp, I urge you to keep reading. It will make sense eventually. Also, after finishing this book, another second reading is also suggested to properly familarise yourself with the concept)

For the other points, favourite activities, socialising, being kind, love, good human being etc. can also be omitted as there is no strong trigger for us to build.

Then, "Receiving compliments from others" is something which we can incorporate with our offering. People who ride a bicycle are generally complimented by others. We can try to create a trigger out of this.

The last one is also another interesting point which is "Surprise". People love getting surprised and love to "surprise" others. This criteria usually works with people having spouses or loved ones. Maybe we can create a trigger with this as well.

So, if we go to our trigger list, we can add two more to the list after the last item (number 5) which are:

6. **(Sex)** A trigger that shows how riding a bicycle regularly improves peoples' sexual ability such as increased libido, lasting and mood. The hook can be a good looking happy romantic couple with scientific statistics supporting the point.

7. **(Compliment)** A trigger that shows other people complimenting the act of riding a bicycle. The hook can be

an image where other people are staring at a group of people riding bicycles with admiration. Here the image itself is enough. No need to add any text.

8. **(Surprise)** A trigger that tells the visitors about the surprise they can give to their spouse. It can only be a text.

A round of applause! We finished a very important task here.

Now, we are very close to creating triggers in the app that generates an addictive experience in the app.

These 8 triggers are the most important parts in your website/app business. You can use these everywhere. In your marketing campaign, your app, website copy, billboards, magazines, case studies, press articles everywhere.

Every time you talk about your business idea to your investors or on stage, start with these trigger points by talking about an impact your business is making.

Your storytelling and your app's offering will be so addicting that everyone will want to be part of that.

We have one final step though, before going to the next part of creating an addictive experience, which is, we have to shortlist the triggers. Yes, those 8 triggers are all amazing.

All those 8 triggers have the power to hook its intended audiences by attracting them with the app's offerings, by generating dopamine, serotonin and endorphin within their brain, making them more happy, calm and relaxed and making them very excited to take action.

Still, among the 8 triggers, there are some triggers which we can actually blend into 1 trigger, to make it even more powerful.

It's like Thanos (from the Avengers). The more rings he collected the more powerful he became. Likewise, if we can blend more triggers into one, that's more power.

That way, we will get the audience so hooked, that even outside distractions can't take their focus away. Therefore, if there is a possibility to combine more than one hook into one, be sure to do that!

This is your chance to create a magical experience for your visitors.

From the list:

- Trigger 1 (Physical activity) and Trigger 6 (Sex) can be created into one trigger.
- Trigger 4 (Productivity) and Trigger 5 (Stress management) can be one trigger.

These combined triggers, we can call our "Power Trigger".

Please note, all the 8 triggers are important. You should not solely focus on the power triggers.

Let me show you how I would design the triggers:

Get fit & better at sex

Riding a bicycle on a daily commute found effective in getting fit and being better at sex! It saves gas money too!

13,456 people found in your city who goes to work everyday riding a bicycle, saving gym time & gas money.

The first trigger I worked on was the trigger combining trigger 1 and trigger 6.

The title says all "Get fit & better at sex"

The images give the visitor the idea about a couple having a good time together followed by some images of cycling activities.

(Fig 3.9 Trigger in bike rental app)

The underlying message here is "Cycling = Happy & fit couple". This makes visitors excited about them. Their brain starts generating Dopamine.

Something that makes a visitor hooked.

Then the call to action button (easily accessible to the visitors' thumb) says "Join Now", which is further telling "13,465 people found in your city who go to work everyday riding a bicycle, saving gym time & gas money".

The underlying message is "other people are doing this, so should you. Be part of this". This generates Serotonin.

If you think you don't have such numbers to "socially hook" the visitors, then simply put a testimonial (not necessarily, that has to be an actual user) of someone with a good avatar and quote, that says something related to the context.

Let's make the second power trigger on the next page:

Cycling before work boosts productivity by 35% and enhances performance.

Several study suggests that doing cardio exercises such as cycling, enhances productivity and reduces stress.

Join Now

13,456 people found in your city who goes to work everyday riding a bicycle, saving gym time & gas money.

I hope you already got the idea.

For this trigger, I am not going to explain everything, as I want to leave it to you to determine what part of this interface is doing what.

(Fig 3.10 Trigger in bike rental app)

Congratulations!

You have successfully completed the most important part of the book. Whether you design the app or you hire a UI & UX designer, I wanted to make sure, you as a founder (or a product designer), know what you want, so that you can give clear instructions to your designers or help yourself build it.

This will surely generate an addictive experience to the visitors' mind.

There is one more thing to do, btw.

Let me ask you a question. Do you know? What is the most powerful feature of any car in the world?

Just think, what is the most powerful feature of a car?

What makes a car, the most powerful tool/item that is so popular that almost everyone in this world relies on the tool called "Car"?

If you think it's the convenience of "travelling", you are partly right. But that's not the correct or exact answer.

If you think it's "speed", that's also a partially correct answer.

Let me tell you the answer. The most powerful feature of any car is "its ability to brake".

It's this feature, relying on which, we trust the car and drive everyday.

Just imagine, there is no brake. Would anyone ever dare to drive any car? Well, this time you know the answer. It's that obvious.

For triggers, the same principle is applicable. If you make your website or app full of triggers then it becomes like the car that does not know when to stop. Because, if you do proper research, you are already ahead in the game. After that, if you place triggers at suitable places within the app/website, that's enough for you to become successful in your app / website business.

But if you overdo this, the addiction experience will break down and the "magical experience" won't last and your visitors will go away.

Therefore, a careful observation is required in order to determine, where to put the triggers and where not to.

My friend, that takes us to the third part of creating Addictive User Experience. Let's go.

Put triggers at the right place only. Failing to do so will take the magical experience away!

At this stage, if you think, why am I using the "Bike Rental App" example for all these important lessons, it's because the Bike Rental App is bringing some complex scenarios for us to discuss and brainstorm which is making my topics more interesting and insightful for you.

Besides, it doesn't matter what example I use, because if you learn the concepts and the lessons I am sharing here, you can implement those in your app or website projects too!

So, as I've said in the previous chapter, the most important feature or functionality of a car is its brake system. Because the brake system lets us stop the car whenever & wherever we want.

Similarly, our triggers should have a brake system. We should know where and when to show the triggers. Only then, we'll be able to get its full benefit.

Placing triggers everywhere will generate a dull experience for your visitors and won't work eventually. It also destroys your brand image.

Therefore, as a founder, you should focus on the user journey of the app.

For those who do not know what a "user journey" is, it is a flow diagram of the user's journey within the app that gives us a visual representation of what screen of the app will be presented to a user at what stage of his/her journey.

If it is still a confusion to you, no worries. I will soon show you the "user journey" of our bike rental app example and how it looks. User journey is an important step in designing experience for your app, therefore it holds immense importance.

Surprisingly & sadly, very few founders I have worked with give importance to the "User Journey" part of an app.

As a founder and especially if you are in the beginning of your app business, designing "User Journey" is even more important. When you grow bigger, you may have your project manager or product owner to take care of things like this.

Don't worry, you don't need to create it.

But you need to know that there is a thing called "User Journey" and how it affects your planning.

To successfully place triggers, we need to create a "User Journey".

You can think of "User Journey" as a map of the user's experience. It helps you better strategize your decisions by creating clarity and transparency among team members.

Creating a user journey is very simple and easy. Just ask yourself, these questions:

1. What are the ways the user learns about our app that directs them to open/install the app or visit the website?

2. After opening the app/website for the first time, what options do the users have? How does the transition from one screen (or page) to another screen (or page) happen? How will the user acquire the service we are offering?

3. If the user is an already existing user, then how will the users navigate?

Let's create the scenarios by answering those above questions for our bike rental app:

1. A user may encounter our bike rental stations (Let's say, we have bike renting stations placed in many different parts of the city) on his/her way and may become interested in riding a bicycle. Then s/he will install the app and will try to rent a bicycle.

2. A user may see our social media ad, or get our marketing emails and may want to install the app from there.

3. A user may visit our app's website and from there, they may want to install & use the app.

4. A user may already be an existing user who rented our bicycle before. S/he may want to open the app again to use the app to rent a bicycle on his/her way home or workplace.

Based on that, let's see, how the user journey looks like:

(Fig 3.11: User journey map)

Let's now observe how the user journey looks like. I know it looks very small to your eyes but for the time being, just understand that, the rounded rectangles (on the left) represent the beginning of the user journey with our app.

The square boxes represent each individual screen of the app.

The emojis underneath each screen represents the user's possible emotional state at that particular screen. If you check, you will see that there are 7 emojis in total for all the 7 screens. There are basically three main emojis. This emoji "●" means the user's emotional state is "confused". This emoji "●" represents "neutral" and this emoji "●" represents a happy state of emotion.

In real life, the user flow is more complex than what I created. It also incorporates, "user login", "user registration", "user authentication", "user authentication failed", "forgot password" etc. multiple if-else scenarios.

But I don't want to bore you with those details as this may take our attention away from the core objective of this chapter, which is to "find the right place to put triggers".

Anyways, let's discuss the strategies with the user journey map with more clarity. Check the zoomed in version of the user journey from belo:

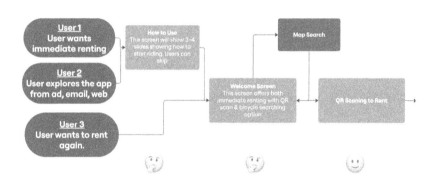

(Fig 3.12: User journey map - part 1)

As we can see, there are three groups of users. The first user is someone who wants to rent a bicycle immediately. Maybe s/he encountered a bike rental station and now wants to immediately rent.

The second user here has seen ads, emails or maybe learnt about the app from a friend and installed the app only for the sake of exploring.

The third user is familiar with the app, used it before and wants to use the app again.

Remember, based on your business model, the beginning of the journey can be different. It depends on how you are designing your businesses too!

For instance, here, just because we've decided to place bike rental stations in the public spots in direct display to the people, it created a new "starting point" in the user journey. Therefore, we've addressed this scenario in the user journey map (as identified by the first user).

As a founder, you should either be able to decide on those journeys or demand from your designer/s to show the journey in his/her design proposal.

Now let me ask you a question. Do all those three users need any trigger in the first screen?

The answer is "NO"!

This is where the "Brake" analogy of cars should come into play.

For instance, the third user, who wants to rent a bicycle again, do we need to show him/her any trigger? Of course not.

Because that user has already rented a bicycle before. S/he is already hooked. Rather, if we further show her/him any "trigger" - we are at the risk of disrupting his/her experience. This is why we are directing him/her to the welcome screen of the app (bypassing the "how to use" screen) so that s/he can directly rent a bicycle. It's a very simple process, but profoundly powerful.

Now, for the first two users, who are both new, one wants to immediately rent (user 1) and another one is just randomly exploring (user 2) are undergoing a different journey than the user 3.

The app shows both of the first two users' "how to use" screens. "How to use" can be alternatively called a "Tutorial" or "Onboarding" screen. This is the stage **where the first time visitors are confused.** If you see the emoji icons below the screen (in Fig 3.12). It shows the "confused" state.

Whenever we find this confused state of emotion of the visitors' we have to understand that this is a perfect spot to place triggers.

Almost all sorts of apps in the marketplace use the "onboarding" screens to educate the first time users. Yet, they miss the point to place triggers there. In your app project, I am sure you also have a plan on what to show in your onboarding or how to use screens. Incorporating "triggers" in those screens can be a game changer.

For instance, in the "how to use" screen, maybe we need to educate the users about how to scan QR codes of the bicycles to start renting, how to unlock a bicycle and how to start riding. While educating them, we need to add some triggering sentences, use relatable powerful triggering images there too.

It's another simple process, but very very powerful.

Now once the first two users pass the how to use screen, they are taken to the "Welcome" screen of the app (As shown in the user journey map in Fig 3.12).

This is how the "welcome screen" looks like:

(Fig 3.13 Welcome screen - bicycle rental app)

Look at the welcome screen.

It is offering the visitors an option to scan and ride. It also has another button called "or search nearby bicycle" so that if somebody is not near to any bicycle point, s/he can search nearby bicycle renting station.

Now let me ask you another question, should we add any trigger here or not?

Remember, this is the welcome screen. This is

a screen where all the three users come and take action.

If your answer is "No", then you are wrong.

Because, although user 1 may be super interested in renting immediately, user 2 still needs nurturing.

The emotional state here is also "confused" if you check the journey map (Fig 3.12).

If you check the user journey map and ask, "wait, why is the emotional state confused in the welcome screen? User 3 is not confused here because user 3 has already used the app before?"

You are right to ask that question!

The answer is, we always focus on the worst existing emotion if there are multiple emotions found. Let's analyse all the 3 users' emotions here on the "Welcome screen":

User 1	Excited
User 2	Confused
User 3	Neutral

Here, as we can see User 1 encountered a bike rental station and user 1 is excited to rent immediately.

User 2 is "confused". It is normal because the user has come to the app from an ad. S/he is not fully aware of the benefit of the app. S/he is not fully hooked.

User 3 is neutral because s/he already used the app before. The welcome screen does not bring any confusion (if not happiness) to him/her.

Therefore, the lowest emotion here is "confused". Therefore, overall, the final emotion for the welcome screen is "confused".

Therefore, we need to place a trigger here.

However, we need to be sure that the trigger we place is not too loud. Because, we don't want to disrupt the experience of the user 3.

I call those "not too loud" triggers "silent triggers". Silent triggers are very very helpful and powerful. I love silent triggers.

Let's add a silent trigger to this screen and see how it looks:

(Fig 3.14 Silent trigger in welcome screen)

I added a testimonial here.

It's just a simple text which is not taking too much real-estate of the mobile display. The image is also very small.

Also, it is not begging for much attention, it just stays there. This is what I call "Silent Trigger".

While adding this silent trigger, I realised, I should place the "Scan & Ride" option to the bottom, near to the thumb.

Now, say somebody scans a bicycle by clicking on the "Scan & Ride" button. We may show a scanning screen after that. The emotion here is "neutral" as we can see in the user journey map in

Fig 3.12. Therefore, there is no need to add any trigger in that screen according to our brake analogy.

Let's jump into the next part of the user journey:

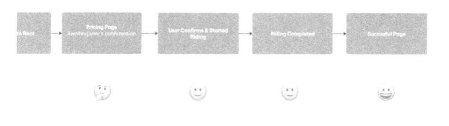

(Fig 3.15: User Journey - Part 2)

So, after the QR Code scanning is finished, when the app verifies that the scanning is valid, it takes the users to the pricing page.

(**Please note:** Dear reader, the decision of the pricing page here is something which entirely depends on your business model, research and many different factors relating to your app idea. Please consider this as just an example and only focus on the core topic here. Yes, if you think, for your app, the pricing page should be somewhere else, feel free to go ahead. There is no right formula.

But it is always a good idea to give the visitors a brief idea of what the app or website does before taking them to the pricing page. Again, this is something which everyone can do right. So, not going to talk about this decision :).)

(Fig 3.16 - Power trigger in pricing page)

In the pricing page, the emotional state is confused again (Fig 3.15). Most of the customers leave the app at this stage.

Therefore, we need some serious triggers here. Something which we called previously "Power Trigger", if you can remember.

Please check the pricing page and read all the texts.

If you check this design of the pricing page, which comes after scanning the bicycle, the small texts below the "Start Riding" button and the blog article below the bicycle image are triggers.

These graphics and images make the visitors trust this process more.

They may feel confused paying $6.99 at first and many thoughts may come to their mind.

However, the article that says "Cycling before work boosts productivity by 35% and enhances performance" is a very strong trigger that has a high potential of generating dopamine in professional users' minds. So they may think less and feel more relaxed. Chances are high some of the users become excited. As a result, their conscious mind will not go against this offering.

Any professional person will start to think, "hum! I will work faster and I will be very proactive in meetings". Instead of thinking about "oh! It's $6.99! I rather go by bus" they will come up with different justification to actually pay for the app.

Another powerful trigger I've placed here is just right below the "Start Riding" button. It's a very small text that says, "13,456 people found in your city who go to work everyday riding a bicycle, saving gym times & gas money".

This information reduces the confusion of the user by telling him/her that other professional people are also using bicycles to go to work. It's a Serotonin booster that makes the visitors' more relaxed and helps them trust the app more.

The better the trigger here, the more people will pay here.

Continuous research is needed to determine what type of trigger works best. A very good way to start is to find out what thoughts may come to the users' mind during this process.

Some visitors/users may think, "What's the point for only riding 10-15 minutes? If I ride this for 30 minutes, that's a lot of money"

You may put some text (with image of course) that shows how 10-15 minutes of bicycle riding daily reduces a person's biological age.

Of course & of course (I can't stress this enough) put real and authentic information from authentic sources. Of course, mention the source name as well. Never ever try to lie here. If they ever find out that you're lying, that's going to cost all the effort and they are never going to trust you ever again.

Having said that, the article I used in this screen is just a demo (it's not real). I just gave you an example of how it will look. I am sure you will find better examples which are authentic for your web or app's pricing page based on your deep user persona.

Now, once the user clicks on the "Start Riding" button, the app asks to put credit card info, which I am going to skip sharing because you know, nothing much for me to add value in those screens. Everyone can do those.

After providing the credit card info, the user starts riding the bicycle. At that moment, the app can show the users a timer, or a map, identifying location to park the bicycle etc. (again those are just regular flow of UI design so I will skip those).

Finally, once the user finishes the ride and successfully parks the bicycle and presses stop. You shouldn't only show them a success message or thank you message.

This is the stage where a user has successfully completed a transaction with you. Chances are high, the user is very happy now because of riding the bicycle. You should take a chance now.

Because when a visitor or a user is happy and that happiness has been caused by your app or website, a smart app or a website should take that opportunity.

This is the phase, where the user is full of dopamine. Because they have completed a task. They also did physical activity. If you ask them to do something now, they will be more willing to do that.

Most of the apps I know ask to give the app a "Five star" rating at this point with fields to share more feedback. Why not use this moment to give them a discount too?

Something that says "Hurray! You just finished a great ride". Then ask them to give feedback in exchange for a 50% discount for the ride the next time? Tell them that this offer is only available now, so if they don't take this, this will go away. But, since they are busy professionals, chances are high, they may not have enough time to give you feedback now, so put an option that says "I'll take it, remind me, same time tomorrow"

I am not going to describe further, because I have a pretty good idea that you will know the rest.

Chapter 4

Make Visitors Addicted

The products that win are those that form habits. - **Nir Eyal**

We are what we repeatedly do - **Aristotle (384 BC - 322 BC)**

*N*ow that you've learnt the art of creating an addictive user experience in your app/website that hooks your visitors and converts them into actual users by making them interested in taking a desirable action, it is time to ask the fundamental question of this book, to talk about why you are here.

Yes, now you know how to attract visitors and make them hooked. This already gives you some competitive edge in your niche.

But that's half of the equation. The rest half relies on whether or not your visitors who got interested the first time can become interested "again".

See, the internet is full of all those clickbaits, triggering graphics, big promises which are designed to lure visitors' in. Once visitors' are inside, they don't find the value and they leave.

If that's your goal, then you are good already. Because in the previous chapter, we already discussed those emotion generating triggers which make the visitors hooked & interested in taking an action in your app or website.

But if your goal is to not only hook or attract them for the first time only but to make them fall in love with your product so much that **they become a loyal user for life (which I call "Addiction"), then this chapter will help you.**

Therefore, this chapter requires your undivided attention, dedication and a commitment from you. A great deal of dedication is needed from your part in order to make your users keep coming back to you over and over.

"How can we make sure every user keeps coming back, Mahir?", you may ask.

Well, you don't have to make every user a repeat user to be honest. If only 4-5% of users become a repeat user, that's a very good number. (This percentage depends on your specific industry as well)

For example, let's say, you got 100 users who signed up and ordered from your app/website once. I am not saying, all the 100 users need to order again. If you get only 4 users to order you again (that means 4% repeat purchase), that's a good number.

But from a product designing point of view, we should work further to improve this conversion rate to be 5%,6% or 7% conversion or even more. The more conversion we can do, the more successful we are. **Because, that means, your app/website has become a part of your users' life.**

So the bottom line is, we need the visitors to convert into users and then, we want a good portion of those users to keep coming back again and again over and over, like they are addicted!

When I am using the word "addicted", I do not mean any negative meaning by this.

I am addicted to tea, I am addicted to some of my favourite restaurants where I go at least once a month, I am addicted to my favourite persons in my life.

All of those are good addictions.

Your app or website can also be a good addiction for your users and **it should be.**

In this chapter we will talk about this in more detail.

Now, let's jump into the process of "how" should we design the experience of the product in such a way that makes its users come back again and again?

In order to do that, your app/website has to become a part of their daily **habit**.

We all know that habit is something which we unknowingly or unconsciously do. For instance, when you drive a car for the first time, you remain very alert & careful not to make any mistakes. Every time you make a turn, you become a bit nervous, yet thrilled.

But after a while, when you do this over and over for a long period of time, your nervous system does not become that triggered like before. You become able to drive while talking to your friends without missing any turns. The driving activity becomes a background job. Your hands know exactly how much you will have to rotate the steering wheel and once the turn is completed you know exactly how much you have to release the wheel, without even consciously planning or thinking for it.

That's what a habit is like!

Repetition creates habit. If you repeat an activity enough times, it becomes a habit.

This same formula applies when you first want to wake up at 5'o clock in the morning and you need an alarm for that. But once you do this enough times, you realise you wake up at exactly 5'o clock without any help from the alarm.

I am not an expert, nor a coach who is the best person to discuss how habit works. But you will agree with me that repetition is the foundation to create a habit.

Therefore, if you want to make an app or a website that becomes part of your users' daily life i.e. becomes a habit, you have to find a way that makes them come back to your app/website again.

So, the lifecycle of converting your app/website into a habit is something like this:

(Fig 4.1: Action converting into habit)

In the above figure, action means the first action that your app/website intends its users to take.

For instance, if you are creating a chat app, the action is "chatting". If you are creating a "task management system", the action here is "creating task", if your app/website project is an "event management platform", the action here is "creating event" or "buying ticket for events".

For Uber, the action is "book a ride". For Amazon Prime, it is "watch a movie". Hope you've got the idea.

From the figure, the first stage is called the "First Action stage". It is at this stage, when your visitors take their first action with you and sign up. "Addictive User Experience" (as discussed in the previous chapter) helps you in this stage.

The second stage is called the "Repetition stage". If you earn $1 from the first action stage, from the repetition stage, you should be able to earn $10 or more. This is why it is very important!

In the bicycle rental app, we only worked on the "First Action" stage. We did a really good job in doing that.

Now, we need to make sure, those who used the app to rent a bicycle the first time, rent the bicycle the second, third and fourth time and so on.

A very popular concept is, if any person does anything for 21 days, the brain's pathways change and eventually that person becomes habituated with that activity. Some other research suggests that the "21 days" number is just a myth. It depends on the person and the type of activity.

While the debate is going on about what is the exact number of days a person should commit to doing an activity, it is evident that, in order to make something a part of habit, we need to "repeatedly do" this for a good amount of time.

That's a good science for us to use and it brings us to a very crucial section in this chapter.

If you need a break, take a break, but come back with full focus.

Keep your mobile phone silent, tell others that you are in a very important study and you don't want to be disturbed. Then, with a full fresh mind, start reading.

If possible, take note.

Step 1: Design for Repetition

In order to make visitors "addicted", the first step is, we need to "design" for repetition.

A very common mistake most of the founders and even professional & experienced designers make is, they design their product beautifully & uniquely spending countless hours but fail to design it for "Repetition".

Some misconception here are:

1. If the user likes the product, s/he will come back again. We **don't** need to do anything with the product.

2. The Marketing team is sending marketing emails, sending discounts, offers and showing Ads to users, so, **nothing** to do from the Product's side.

3. Product should **only** do the straightforward sign up process and offer functionality of its intended use.

How can we design/build the product for repetition?

Answer: If you are an intelligent reader already, you should know the answer by now then. We should create "triggers" for repetition.

In the last chapter, we created triggers to hook visitors & make them interested to take their "first step" with the app.

Now, we need to create triggers that make the users use the app for the "second time". We can call these triggers "Repetition Triggers".

This is kinda tricky but not impossible. For the sake of showing you the creation process, first, let me show you the difference between the trigger for "repetition" with the trigger for "first action".

First Action Trigger	Repetition Trigger
Designed for "visitors" who are new.	Designed for users who just finished a particular action in the app.
This trigger is placed when the visitor's stage is "confused"	This trigger is placed when the visitor just finished the

and most importantly in the beginning.	first action within the app when they are excited & happy.
This trigger talks about how in general, the product helps the visitors.	This trigger talks about how **repeat** use of this product helps the users.
Focuses on making visitors happy, excited and interested.	Focuses on making visitors happy, excited and interested in **the future.** That's why it's a bit tricky.

Hope you've got a good idea about what is a "Repetition Trigger".

Now, let's see some examples:

Example 1:

Say, you've created a task management SAAS app which works on both website and mobile. A project manager is testing the system for trial use. In order to test the system, s/he created a random task, assigned the task to someone from the organisation and then randomly wrote some notes. Then s/he clicks on the "Create Task" button.

A successful message pops up saying, "Congratulations! You've created a task successfully".

While showing that is good. The UI should have an option for creating another new task. Which is something like the example from below:

(Fig 4.2 Trigger for repetition)

Look at the success message on the bottom right, that says "Congratulations", then in the second line "You just created your first task". With a call to action button that says "+ New Task". This button is a "trigger for repetition".

You may think, this trigger is not that persuasive enough. But think, you already placed a lot of "First Action Triggers" during the sign up process. Also, this is a B2B SAAS Task Management App and usually the interfaces are busy for such types of web apps. Therefore, for this particular scenario, this is the best you can do from Product's perspective.

Also, know that, the same product manager who is using your product for 14 days trial is also checking your competitors' task management apps too.

If you do your job well, be sure to receive a response from them like this "Hey, your product is very easy and comfortable to use. Let's sit for further discussion".

I know, because I have received similar responses from tons of trial users for my SAAS app which I designed.

Example 2:

For the bicycle rental app, the "Repetition Trigger" can be like this:

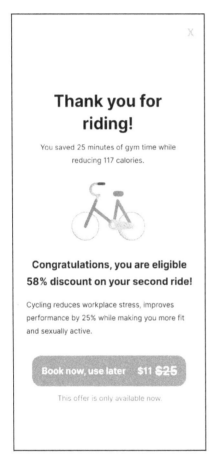

(Fig 4.3: Repetition trigger for the bicycle rental app)

This trigger is more persuasive than the previous example.

Because we could get enough space to craft a beautiful and engaging offer here.

The whole text-copy here is deeply researched.

In the "Book now...." button, the $11 price is shown crossing the $25. A classic textbook science on consumer behavior. It always works.

Finally, "This offer is only available now" creates urgency in the users' mind. Overall, this is a good example of a "Repetition Trigger".

I hope you understand what a repetition trigger looks like.

I know you still may have a lot of doubts about how you may create one for your own app/website.

Here is a list of ideas for you to better understand the concept:

Type of App	Trigger for Repetition
Mindfulness, Yoga, Breathing, Self-help, Sleep, Productivity etc.	After action, show a "Thank you" or "Congratulations" message and give some helpful benefit of the action they just did along with a button to do that again.
E-commerce app, Food ordering app, Ride sharing etc.	Send them to a thank you page and offer them a discount on their next order.
Any kind of management system (such as task, accounts, operation, inventory etc.)	In the thank you or success alert, show a button to do that again. If possible add some value they will get if they click on the button. It can be productivity, improvement, or

	anything.
Any social app (dating, networking, chatting, conference etc.)	Once they send a friend request, message, or register for an event, show a thank you alert with further option to do it again and incentivise the user.
Any learning platform	Once a student enrolls into a course or watches a video of any course instructor, show a thank you message with some data showing how further learning can help the user with the option to do it again.

Hope you've got an idea of this concept. However, I would like to emphasize the fact that creating a Repetition Trigger is only possible if you've researched on the user persona, found their common words, and researched on their problems.

We did this process in Chapter 3 when we determined our "one right" user group and then talked with them.

Without doing any prior research, survey and/or interview, your triggers can't be strong. You may make an attempt, but it will lack strong use of words & relatable images that will fail to grab the attention of your users. A classic mistake most of the founders & designers make.

(If you understand this, then well done. Now, let's go to the second part of making visitors addicted. Remember, my suggestion for taking note is still on)

Step 2: Get Rid of Dopamine Killers from Your App

This is another crucial step in creating your product that makes visitors addicted. Let me tell you what I mean by this.

Say, you've signed up for a gym near your home where you are planning to go at least 4 days a week. At the beginning, you were very excited, "yay! now I will be doing regular exercise and I will be very fit" you thought. Not only that, in your mind, you had imagined yourself as the best good looking version of you wearing beautiful clothes which you had been wanting to wear for a long time.

After hitting the gym for a few days, one day, you said to yourself, "nah, it's very far. I don't feel like walking today". So you skipped that day. Then, after going to the gym for a few more days, you skipped another day because you realised your gym clothes were dirty. Then you skipped again and realised, you don't enjoy going to the gym anymore.

For the first few days, you were very excited but as the day progressed, you realised going to the gym requires some preparation such as walking/driving to the gym, taking an extra pair of clothing, carrying a bag and drinking protein shake or healthy drinks before going to the gym which you started not liking at all. Those simple redundant tasks grew on you.

At the eve of every new year, millions of people, full of dreams, full of energy, full of ambition, full of dopamine and excitement, get into the gym only to discover a few months later that they are no longer excited.

My dear friend, this small incident needs a thorough investigation, because, if you understand the science of "why" people stop doing something which once made them excited, you will do things differently with your app project, because this may happen with your app too! We need to prevent this.

A very good science is available here for us to use. Let me explain.

When a person joins the gym for the first time, she or he is inspired by having a beautiful and healthy body which generates dopamine in their brain. So they join a gym and they enjoy the first few weeks as they are full of dopamine in that period of time.

But as time progresses, frequent disruptions in the process, for instance, going to the gym, carrying a bag for extra clothes, changing clothes etc. the boring tasks come in the way which start making the gym experience very unpleasant.

It's like a very long "Ad" in an interesting movie. The first few times, you patiently wait for the ad to go away. But as the Ad keeps coming back, your interest to watch the movie goes away. Eventually, you stop watching the movie and save yourself by engaging in a new activity.

The same thing happens with millions of people who stop going to the gym. If you look at the figure below, it shows how those small, repeating and boring tasks diminish our energy level and excitement as the time progresses.

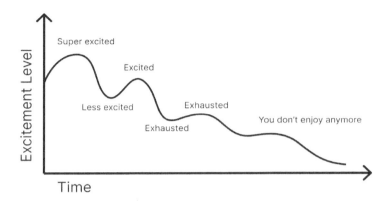

(Fig 4.4: Boring tasks diminishes peoples' enjoyment)

Your app has those "excitement killers" (or "dopamine killers") too!

Most of the founders & product designers spend most of their time brainstorming what new features can be implemented that may attract the users. While introducing "new features" is important, you should also focus on making the user journey very comforting & easy.

You do that by getting rid of the "experience killers" in your app.

In our gym example, the experience killers were "walking or driving to the gym", "getting ready for the gym", "carrying bags, clothes etc. for the gym" etc.

For your app or web project, it can be anything, no matter what type of app or web project you are building.

Identifying "experience killer" or "dopamine killer" is very easy but the problem is, you are so much accustomed with your app's interface that it becomes almost impossible for you to identify those experience killer elements or functionalities in your app.

Therefore, it is important you do another round of an interview with someone who is within your target user group but haven't signed up yet.

If you suddenly start feeling "oh! Come on, this book is making me do so much work." inside your mind, then let me tell you "It is very normal to feel this way. But there is one secret. It's actually a very easy task. I mean, if you've already come this far, then compared to all those challenging tasks you did previously, this task is not that complicated.

Also, the reward is very high."

One common argument against "doing the interview" in this step is, "we are already testing the app with our team members, friends & family members". So we know where the app is becoming poor in experience.

Well, I am not talking about common issues such as, "slow loading", "wrong input field errors", "app crashes", "inactive button" etc. Those are very easy. Everyone can solve those. You do not need to interview users to identify these issues. I know this.

You need to interview users to identify experience issues that only "a user" can find.

Let me share a real life example with you.

In 2018, after multiple failures, we eventually built a "Delivery Management App for ecommerce focused delivery companies". We had one right group of target users, which was "delivery companies".

Our product had some key features:

A delivery company could sign up, add team members, add riders, add merchants (customers), take orders from their merchants and change the status of orders from "Pending" to "Successfully

Delivered". It was not a full-fledged delivery app at that moment, but it was good enough to add value to the delivery companies.

We did bug testing, removed slow loading experience and got rid of unnecessary form fields etc to enhance user experience for the app. We told all the team members (6 at that time) to share the app with their friends and family members insisting they test it and provide feedback.

Everyone praised the app. No bugs were reported, and the app worked as expected. However, after onboarding the first real delivery company, we received feedback that completely changed our perspective.

The delivery manager mentioned, "Changing order statuses one by one takes too much time. Sometimes we need to update hundreds of orders at once."

Not only that, he kept saying, "Also, when I add a rider, the app waits for the rider to accept the invitation from their email. But most riders get lost in the process and say they can't find how to log in. Can you make a simple login system where I just give them a URL and password so they can directly access orders and change statuses?"

Wow! We never thought that. Especially, who could possibly think that the riders would get lost in the process of signup? Everyone knows how to click the "Accept Invitation" button from an email and then just follow the process, right? Haha, the reality was far different.

We asked further questions to understand why the riders can't login? and learnt "the most bizarre yet it still happens" story from the delivery manager.

He said, "Actually, they don't have access to their email. They bought their smartphones from someone else and that smartphone had the previous owners' email address already signed. When I sent an invitation to their "actual" email address, they wanted to login to their own email address but they say they forgot the password of their own email address."

I was taking a very long deep breadth hearing the scenario. The delivery manager kept saying, "So, I realised, it's better if I just send them a login URL and password which I can set up for each and individual rider. Can you do that please?".

I hope you understand the scenario now!

The feedback revealed two critical "experience killers" that none of us had anticipated.

How many times we tested the app, talked to them!

Even after finally launching the app, we ourselves did testing first and never anticipated such feedback would come from them!

It's not our fault and of course not theirs.

Some discussions, ideas and feedback only come when your users use the app for the first time, because they are also new in the process.

We immediately introduced a bulk status update feature, allowing users to update multiple orders simultaneously. Additionally, we simplified the rider login system by enabling managers to share a URL and password, eliminating the need for email invitations.

This update suddenly made the app more addictive because it eliminated two major friction points in the user journey.

The key lesson here is that certain experience killers are invisible to you but highly frustrating for your users. Interviews with real users—especially those within your target group—help you identify and fix these issues.

So, what should you do next?

Find at least five people from your target user group who haven't used your app yet. Ask them to complete specific tasks within your app while observing their behavior and listening to their thoughts. Don't help them unless absolutely necessary. Note the moments when they hesitate, get confused, or show signs of frustration—these are your experience killers.

Once you've gathered enough feedback, prioritize fixing these issues before adding new features. Remember, no matter how innovative your features are, they won't matter if the core experience is frustrating.

Eliminating experience killers is what makes your app not only functional but also irresistible. PERIOD!

Step 3: Make Your App Behave Like a Human

Imagine, you and your friend walk into a restaurant. The atmosphere is warm, the staff greets you with a smile and they say, "Welcome! We're so happy to have you here!"

Then they guide you to a table, hand you a menu and give you some complimentary food. What's your feeling here?

Now imagine the opposite. You walk in and the restaurant feels cold and uninviting. The staff doesn't acknowledge you. So you and your friends sit at a table and finally when you get their attention, you ask for the menu and they hand you a menu without saying a word. How would you feel now?

Well, most of the apps or websites on the internet are like this. Why? Because nobody cares. All the humans including me who use the internet on planet earth accepted the fact that apps/websites can behave like robots and since we've accepted this, most of the founders hardly put an effort to make their product humane.

There lies your opportunity to create an addictive experience!

Among both restaurants, which restaurant will you visit next time? Obviously, the first one!

Now, if your product can somehow offer the same experience as the first restaurant, where do you think your visitors or users will come back again and again?

You know the answer!

Your app should communicate in a way that feels like users are interacting with a friendly human, not a robotic interface. One of the most effective ways to achieve this is through the tone of your language and the use of visual elements like emojis.

A friendly tone with elements like a fist bump (🤜), a hug (🫂), a wink (😉), or a wave (👋) can create a sense of warmth and familiarity. These small additions may seem trivial, but they trigger the release of oxytocin in the brain, the same hormone responsible for feelings of connection and trust.

If you think, putting emoji and using a friendly tone is "just" another usual design advice found online, then know that, it's not.

Research shows that physical touch, like hugging, produces oxytocin in the brain, making people feel loved and connected. Interestingly, even talking about a hug or seeing a "hug" icon can generate a similar emotional response. This is because our brains react to symbols and words as if they were real experiences.

Let me give you an example that is fun!

Imagine there's a fresh lemon in front of you. It has a bright yellow skin, smooth yet slightly bumpy to the touch. You pick it up and bring it close to your nose—the sharp, tangy citrus aroma instantly fills the air, awakening your senses. You take a knife and slowly slice it open. As the blade cuts through, tiny droplets of lemon juice spray into the air, releasing an even stronger burst of citrus fragrance.

You pick up one of the slices. It glistens with fresh juice, the pulp exposed, radiating a vibrant yellow. Now, imagine taking a bite. The sourness hits your tongue immediately, making your mouth involuntarily pucker. Your saliva glands activate, flooding your mouth with moisture, trying to balance the sharp tang of the lemon.

Did you feel it? That slight tingling sensation? Maybe even a little more saliva in your mouth? That's the power of the brain. Just by imagining the lemon, your body reacted as if it were real. This happens because when you think about something, your brain processes it as if it's real.

We can use this psychological effect in your app. By integrating the right words, icons, and interactions, we make the experience more human-like and engaging.

Instead of displaying a dull "Error" message, your app can say, "Oops! Something went wrong. Let's fix it together! 🤝"

This handshake icon generates a feeling of "handshake" in the visitors' or users' minds. A very small change but this can completely shift the user's emotional response, making them feel supported rather than frustrated.

Just like how a good restaurant experience makes customers want to return, a humanized app experience makes users want to keep coming back.

By applying these human-centered design principles, your app will not only be functional and frictionless but also deeply engaging and emotionally resonant. The more human your app feels, the more users will trust, enjoy, and return to it.

Let's get back to one of our previous design examples, and make that more humane!

(Fig: 4.5 Comparison between designs with & without humane experience)

Hope you remember from chapter 3, when we were auditing some of the popular apps from the app store when I finally created the first screen of a financial app designed for professionals. At that moment, I only placed a trigger to hook its intended audience without adding any humane experience. That's the first screen here.

The second screen here is giving a humane experience!

I hope you can differentiate which one is more welcoming, engaging and putting you at ease.

The bottom line is, if your app has a friendlier tone, it will definitely make your visitors & users more engaged. They will love to keep coming back. Eventually, it will become a part of their habit and without them knowing, they will become a regular user.

Now tell me, what's stopping you from creating an engaging and addictive user experience in your project?

Chapter 5

The 3rd Level of Building Product

*You've got to start with the customer experience and work backwards to the technology. - **Steve Jobs (1995 - 2011)***

*C*ongratulations! You are almost at the end of this book and there is just one more thing I want to share. From chapter 1 to chapter 4, I've only shared some secrets and methodologies with you. I wanted to share the mistakes I did, so that you as a founder do not repeat the same mistakes.

But this chapter is a little bit different. The topic this chapter covers is rather spiritual than practical. Therefore, there is no "structure" or "method" in this chapter. In fact, a very separate book is needed for this chapter.

First question, what is 3rd level? We have to understand this concept first.

Let's say, you started learning a new language. Say, it's called the "Language A". You are now memorising the different vocabulary, the vowels, the letters, the sounds of each letter and practicing writing each letter of the language.

You know that you are only a beginner in your journey of learning the language A. We can call this the beginner stage or level 1.

After a few months, you are comfortable speaking this language and you can construct meaningful sentences with it. But still you are not fully confident. We can call this level 1.5.

Finally, after 1 year of practice, you become an expert in the language. You are comfortably fluent and your pronunciation has also improved. You sound like a native speaker.

Not only that, now you know which words you should omit when you speak, which words you should emphasize and all those different sounds with the same words. When you speak, you can translate your own language to the language A and you can perfectly deliver any thought in language A.

We can call this level 2.

If level 1 is the "beginner" level, then level 2 is the "expert" level.

Now, one day, you married a person from the country where Language A is widely spoken. You created a family together and you have a baby daughter born in that country.

At the age of 4, your daughter starts speaking the language A, even more fluently and perfectly than you. What took you years of practice and learning became inherently natural to your daughter and you are always very much exhilarated to see that!

So, your child is not at the "beginner" stage of that language of course. Your child is not an "expert" too, because your child is not following any "rulebook". She actually looks like a beginner because most of the time what she says doesn't make any sense.

But whatever she says is so perfect and eloquently pronounced that you can't think she is at her "beginner" stage.

My dear friend, get introduced with level 3.

Some key properties of level 3 is:
i) It very much looks like level 1.
ii) Level 3 doesn't play by the rules.
iii) Level 3 follows what the heart says.

Now, use this analogy to the industry legends, timeless business titans, visionary entrepreneurs, elite group of artists and super successful professionals. You will find many people from level 3. But outwardly they just look like they are amateurs.

Level 3 is something which is hard to grasp in the beginning but the more you look in the real world, you will find plenty of examples of level 3.

What happens when a person starts learning something? We can call this person a beginner (level 1) right? After many years, when the person becomes an expert, we can say, s/he reached "level 2". One day, that person realised "s/he actually knows nothing" and therefore s/he decided s/he "needs to learn more". S/he also realised, all those "rulebooks" don't matter anymore. So s/he started playing by what his/her heart says and s/he became famous because everyone started loving him/her. That is level 3.

The funny similarities of level 1 and level 3 is, both of them acknowledge that they don't know anything.

Level 3 is a very mysterious stage. It exhibits a very illusionary presence of a person being at level 1 while the person is actually operating from level 3.

Because, people from level 1 know that there is a rulebook but they don't know the rules, so they don't play by the book. On the other hand, people from level 3 don't "need" the rulebook and therefore they too, don't play by the book.

On the other hand, there are some key differences between level 2 and level 3:

i) Level 2 is always very rules focused. Level 3 knows nothing matters as long as they are stuck to what the heart says.

ii) Level 2 is logical. Level 3 is artistic.

iii) Level 2 follows the rulebook. Level 3 follows their heart and what they do becomes part of the rulebook.

I know that the topic is already touching spiritual points and you've started to think about many questions, let me put a stop here, and just give you the bottom line here by cutting it short,

"You don't have to always play by the rulebook. Follow your intuition and be bold enough to build amateur products that look stupid"

Most of the founders and designers find it difficult to fully express their creativity because of the fear of being mediocre. That is the common fear of anyone operating from Level 2.

An expert's greatest fear is other people taking them as an amateur. This sabotages their creative expression.

So, when most of the founders or designers start creating an app, the first step that they do is to copy other similar apps from the marketplaces. That's a proven formula I know. In most of the cases, common designs win the audience because the audience finds it easy.

However, a situation may come, where you may have to step out of the rulebook and be bold.

Maybe just a white screen with a very ordinary sign up form is what is needed. Nobody will understand the fact that you've spent hours researching the simple sign up form and decided to make it very "blank". Nobody needs to know. If it works, it works.

It was the end of 2015. We were trying to build a location based social media app. We named it Landknock Social.. The idea was to show its users a map with his/her real time location on map. In the map, users would be able to click on other people or objects and interact with them. If a person wanted, s/he could chat with other people as well.

So the concept was simple. There were two features: chatting feature and map feature, right? This is how the app looked in the beginning:

(Please go to the next page)

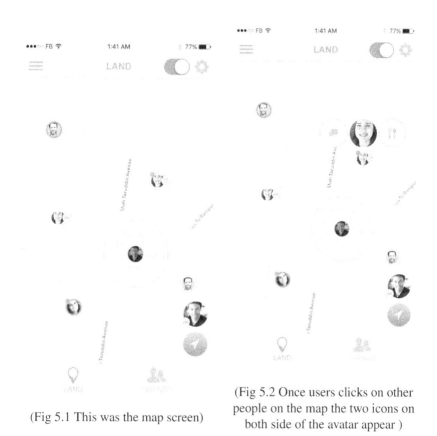

(Fig 5.1 This was the map screen)

(Fig 5.2 Once users clicks on other people on the map the two icons on both side of the avatar appear)

In the above two screen UI, the left one shows you all the people around you. If you click on someone around you, the two icons appear as shown in the second screen. One is for chatting and another one is for checking the person's activity.

If you click on the "chat" icon. The app would take you to the chat interface.

(Fig 5.3: Chat screen)

The above design is very simple, professional and it meets 100% of the requirements of this project. It is elegant, useful and cool.

But the problem is, the users who come to this app have a very particular need in their mind. They want to stay on the map.

So, I created something that challenged me in all possible ways. Now I know that, I operated from level 3 that moment.

Let me show you what I designed:

The map was the same as before

Interaction was the same as before

When it comes about chatting, instead of taking users to another page, users chat on the map staying at the same place within the app.

As hours passed by, I became less confident and wanted to go back to the old version of the design.

(Fig 5.4: Chatting possible on map)

Still, I wanted to test and launch the new update.

At that moment the app had only around 100 users with daily active 8-10 users.

With that release, we got a few hundreds more downloads and suddenly the number of active users jumped from 10 to 50+. People loved the in-map chatting feature so much that they started doing it more and more.

That was the first time I met my level 3 designer self.

This idea was stupid, confusing and rewarding and most importantly it came to me rather than me actively searching for it.

Lesson to learn from this example is, don't get scared to design unconventional designs which may not look similar to what other apps/websites are doing. Don't worry if you are worried that your users may find your app "boring".

If you've done your research right, just follow what your heart says. Don't overdo it though. Take one little step at a time, test it and then go further.

Final Notes

You are an innovator! You are the future. What you are building has real value to the planet earth. You deliver true, genuine and tangible value to your users/customers or visitors. This is why, if people sign up at your app/website, they keep coming back.

Your customers love you and they are loyal to your offerings!

You are the Picasso.

You are the Leonardo Da Vinci.

You are the Steve Jobs.

Because, when you create, you do not represent yourself. You represent all the best of humanity.

Your creation is a connection between your higher self with God.

This is why I support you.

I wrote this book, just to help you a bit.

Even if this book helps you get closer to 1% of your dream, remember, that's a huge gain. Because, with time, this 1% will give birth to new knowledge, new ideas, new inspiration.

So? What's next?

Now, it's your job to work on your new or existing app project with a goal to make it among the top 1% in your niche.

If there is any research gap, you know what to do.

If there is any feature gap, you know what to do.

If there is any addiction UX gap, you know what to do.

Get excited! Because you are about to make history!

I am proud to be a part of your legendary journey! Let me know your thoughts by emailing me here at iram@landknock.com. It always gives me immense pleasure to hear your journey, experience and thoughts.

You can also visit my website www.mahiriram.com learn more about me & my upcoming books :) At the end of this book, I have nothing but to wish you all the best in your adventure!

You are awesome! Take care!

Mahir Iram,

Mar 16, 2025

New York, USA

P.S: Ah! Beautiful spring is coming. Nature is also creating an addictive experience for its loving users. Green grasses are coming out, to get the first ray of the beautiful sun. I am just a humble addicted user of this nature :)

Bonus Point: The Better Approach To Find The Right User Group for Addictive Experience

Note for the readers:

This is an optional chapter. If you've already determined your "right group of users", you may skip this. But if you are unsure whether or not you are building for the right group of users, or if you are in doubt that maybe there is another user group which may bring you good business and you are not sure which one to go with, I'd say please read this chapter.

Please note, I will just share the key steps leaving out the tiny specific details. So I request the readers, when you read it, keep in mind that many of the situations with your business may be different and you may need to do further research on the topics shared in this chapter to better execute the approach. Just try to understand the basics and apply it to your own different situation.

Let's begin!

First, determine the user groups:

You are doubtful because you can't decide which user group to choose for. It is very common. Especially for the first time founders and/or product designers, it becomes very difficult to go with only one user group because "what if the other user group is better?"

Let's say, you can't decide among two user groups. We can name them user group A and user group B.

Second, design a "fake" landing page for the both the user groups:

I'd suggest hiring a "Landing Page Designer" from popular freelancing platforms like "Upwork" or "Fiverr".

Make sure that the person you hire is skilled in designing landing pages, digital marketing and also has good copywriting skills.

It shouldn't cost you more than $100 to design two landing pages.

If you are one of those founders who can do the digital marketing and sales landing page design, you can do that by yourself too.

Also, popular AI applications can help you build landing pages by yourselves.

You can follow whichever works for you but if you ask me, I'd suggest, it's better to hire someone than trying to do everything by yourself. Make sure to give a deadline of maximum 3 days. With revisions, it shouldn't go for more than 7 days.

Typically, a landing page should have the following structure:

- A catchy headline that resonates with the specific user group. Again, this is just an example. Change it according to your own unique situation. Do not focus on what you do, focus on what the final experience will be.

- Few key points of the problem with their current scenario and how your solution can help them.

- Your app's features with screenshots (The app doesn't have to be published. You can generate random screenshot and put those in the landing page)

- Show some statistics regarding the benefits of what you are offering that resonates with the user group.

- Show a unique value proposition of why your solution is better than the other solutions.

- Call to action buttons.

- Testimonials, feedback from other users. Now that you are in the testing phase, I get that you don't have any actual users. Therefore, the feedback can be fake. (Of course, when you provide an actual offer, make sure to provide real testimonials.)

It is my request to the reader of this book to take a look at similar landing pages from the internet to get an idea about an ideal structure of a landing page.

Since this book focuses on how to create "Addictive UX" in your app or website, I am not going to discuss everything in detail about the "Landing Page" creation process. But get this, this is an important step for you to test whether the user group is "right".

Once you have created two separate landing pages for both the user group A & B, it's time to finally, run two different ads for both the user groups on Facebook/Tiktok/Instagram

Now create and run two ads (one for user group A and one for user group B) on a social media platform (choose only 1 platform) with your offer with the objective of getting traffic to the respective landing pages. Spend an equal amount ($10-$50) for both the Ads.

To make it clear, create an Ad for the user group A and make it a "Traffic" ad (or something similar) so that users can click on the ad and visit your landing page for user group A.

Do the same for the user group B. Create an Ad for the user group B and make the traffic visit to the landing page for user group B.

Once the Ads are published, now it's just a waiting game. Wait for 3-5 days.

After 3-5 days of the ad run, now is the moment of truth.

Ask yourself, based on the total impressions, what percentage of people actually clicked on the Ad? And eventually, among the total clicks on the Ad, how many people clicked on the "Sign Up" or "Download" button or the call to action button?

Let's say, for both the Ads, this is what we find:

Ad	Audiance	Traffic	Impression	# of Visit	CTA Click
Ad A	User Group A	Landing Page A	10,000	995	38
Ad B	User Group B	Landing Page B	11,000	895	12

From the above, we can see that the "Ad A" has the highest number of visits (995) and also the conversion to click is high, 38. That means, 38/995*100 = 3%

For the second ad, among 895 visits, 12 people clicked. That means, 12/895*100 = 1.3%

It is clear that the User Group A is the winner. So there goes your doubt killer.

It gives you enough confidence and answers all of your worries regarding which user group you should go for. Also, you know how much of marketing cost you are saving yourself by going with user group A and how much more you would have ended up paying if you were choosing user group B.

If you have the slightest doubt about the test being unnecessary and if you think even for a second that, this investment of money and time for this test is unnecessary. Let me tell you, one of the most common and fatal mistakes founders make is giving themselves a false boundary of fake urgency and then they rush the processes of building an app/website without doing any proper research.

Some of their common excuses are, "I have to present it to the investors soon" or something like "I have to pitch it at this competition" as if, if they somehow present a faulty product, they are gonna get the money or win the competition. That's classic BS. Don't get offended, I was also one of those founders, so I know :).

If you think about money being wasted in doing the test. I can assure you that going with the wrong user group will cost you more in the long run. Spending $200-$300 for doing such tests is nothing compared to the future losses you would have ended up doing without such tests! That's plain simple.